THE GOVERNORS OF OHIO

THE OHIO HISTORICAL SOCIETY

COLUMBUS

1 9 5 4

Printed by THE STONEMAN PRESS, Columbus

PREFACE

One of the frequent requests made of the Ohio Historical Society has been for information on Ohio's governors. With this in mind, the Society ran a series of brief biographical sketches of the first twenty-four governors in its *Museum Echoes,* a small monthly periodical. The series proved popular, and the suggestion was made that these sketches be combined with those of the rest of the governors into a volume which would be available to schools, libraries, and interested persons. The Ohio Sesquicentennial Commission joined the Society in sponsoring the volume.

Authors of the sketches were selected generally because of special study they have done on the subjects. Authors of the biographies of recent governors, from Davis to Lausche, with the exceptions of those of White and Herbert, are men with intimate personal knowledge of the governors about whom they write and their administrations.

The portraits accompanying the sketches, with the exception of Governor Lausche's photograph, are from the paintings of the governors which hang in the State Capitol. Because the quality of these paintings varies so much, and because a number would reproduce so poorly in their entirety, it was decided to present them uniformly with emphasis on the faces. In other words, the purpose of the pictures is not so much to present the Statehouse paintings as to give the readers an idea of the appearance of each governor.

CONTENTS

AUTHORS

EDWARD TIFFIN
1803 - 1807

The state of Ohio was organized in 1803 from the Northwest Territory after a bitter struggle between the party of Arthur St. Clair, governor of the territory, and the "Chillicothe Junto," which favored immediate statehood for the section east of the mouth of the Great Miami River. The leader of the latter group was Edward Tiffin, who was elected the first governor of the new state.

Edward Tiffin was born in Carlisle, England, on June 10, 1766, and attended the Latin school in that city. At the age of twelve he apprenticed himself as a student of medicine. He completed his apprenticeship in 1783 and came with his parents, Henry and Mary Parker Tiffin, and four brothers and sisters to America, where he settled with them in Charles Town, Virginia, now in Jefferson County, West Virginia. He began the practice of medicine here while still only seventeen years of age, and apparently soon had a sizeable practice.

That he was a respected member of society in his Virginia home is evidenced by the fact that his name is found on the lists of "Gentlemen

Justices'' appointed by the governor of Virginia, and also by the fact that in the late 1780's (the exact date is uncertain) he married Mary Worthington, daughter of a wealthy landowner, Robert Worthington, and sister of Thomas Worthington, who was to become Ohio's sixth governor.

Although reared in the Episcopal Church, Tiffin and his wife came under the influence of the Methodist revival in 1790 and joined the Methodist Church. Two years later Tiffin was ordained a deacon by Bishop Francis Asbury and throughout the rest of his life continued to serve the church as a lay preacher.

Tiffin, like many other Virginians, felt the appeal of the West, and in 1798, emigrating with his family and that of Thomas Worthington and their recently manumitted colored servants, settled in the wilderness village of Chillicothe on the banks of the Scioto River in the Ohio country. Tiffin, who was thirty-two years old at the time, has been described as a vivacious, florid-faced English gentleman of medium height with pleasant manners and extraordinary conversational powers. He had already won considerable reputation as a physician and surgeon. He continued to practice his profession under the trying conditions of the frontier.

Tiffin carried with him from Virginia a recommendation for public office addressed to Governor St. Clair and signed by George Washington. A few months after Tiffin's arrival in Chillicothe the governor appointed him prothonotary of the territorial court of common pleas. This was the beginning of a long public career in Ohio. He served as speaker of the territorial house of representatives, 1799-1801, and as president of the constitutional convention in 1802, where his authority to determine the membership of committees was an important factor in policy-making in that body.

He was elected governor of the newly organized state almost without opposition in 1803 and again in 1805 for a second term. It was during his second term that he received a commendatory letter from President Jefferson for his efficiency in foiling Aaron Burr's expedition. Before the close of his second term he was elected by the general assembly to the United States Senate. He took his seat in 1807 but resigned in March 1809. After the death of his wife in July 1808, he expressed a wish to return to his home near Chillicothe and resume his medical practice and farming.

He did not long remain a private citizen, however, for a few months after his return to Chillicothe he was elected to the Ohio House of Representatives, where he served two terms as speaker, 1809-11. In the fall of 1812 he was appointed by President Madison commissioner of the general land office, an office which had just been created. Tiffin successfully organized the land records, and his foresight saved them from destruction when the British invaded Washington in 1814. In the fall of the same year he secured the approval of the president to exchange offices with Josiah Meigs, then surveyor general for the Northwest, in order to be able to reside at home. Tiffin by this time had remarried and had one daughter. His second wife was Mary Porter, by whom he had four daughters and a son.

Tiffin continued in the office of surveyor general for fifteen years under the administrations of James Madison, James Monroe, and John Quincy Adams, all of whom praised his work. He was relieved of the office only a few weeks before his death.

During the last four or five years of his life Tiffin suffered severe nervous headaches. In spite of that fact he continued to supervise the work of his office and farm and to give his professional services to the poor of the community who called upon him. He died on August 9, 1829, and was buried in Grandview Cemetery at Chillicothe.

Edward Tiffin had had a distinguished and versatile career. He was a skillful physician, an able lay preacher, an efficient and respected public servant, and a man of highest integrity. The city of Tiffin, Ohio, is named in his honor, and the state may well take pride in her first governor.

The Ohio Historical Society   S. WINIFRED SMITH

THOMAS KIRKER
1807 - 1808

When Edward Tiffin resigned the governorship of Ohio in March 1807 to take a seat in the United States Senate, Thomas Kirker, then speaker of the Ohio Senate, became acting governor until December, when Tiffin's term expired. In the election of October 1807, Return J. Meigs, Jr., received a majority of the popular vote over Nathaniel Massie, but the general assembly ruled that Meigs was ineligible because he had not resided continuously in the state for four years prior to the election, as required by the constitution. As a result of the decision Kirker continued as acting governor for the 1807-8 term.

Ohio's second governor was born in Tyrone County, Ireland, in 1760. His father, being unable to make a living for a large family on the poor soil of his native county, brought the family to America when Thomas was nineteen. They settled in Lancaster, Pennsylvania, where in a few years the father died. There is no further record of Thomas until 1790 when he married Sarah Smith, a young woman from a good Lancaster family. Not long thereafter they moved to Kentucky in spite of the hazardous journey and frontier conditions at the journey's end. One account states that they were targets for Indian arrows during the trip.

Kirker left Kentucky (whether for economic reasons or because of opposition to slavery is uncertain) and moved to Manchester, Ohio, around 1793. About two years later he settled on a farm in Liberty Township, Adams County, which was his home for the rest of his life. This is said to have been the first settlement in the county outside a stockade. According to family tradition, the future governor and his wife, leaving their children at home, would take a gun and walk twelve miles through the woods to church and back. From 1808 until his death Kirker was a ruling elder in the Presbyterian church at West Union, as also were four of his five sons. In 1809 he was one of three appointed to receive subscriptions for a stone church building, and his name heads the subscription list.

Kirker became a leading citizen of his community, often called upon by common consent to arbitrate disputes among his neighbors. He was appointed by Governor Arthur St. Clair as a justice of the peace and was therefore a member of the first court of quarter sessions which met at Manchester in 1797. His reputation spread throughout the county, and he was chosen as one of the delegates from Adams County to the first constitutional convention. He represented his county in the lower house of the first general assembly, which met in March 1803. In the fall of 1803 he was elected to the state senate and was reelected to that body for eleven consecutive general assemblies (1804-15), serving as speaker for seven terms.

After the close of the thirteenth general assembly Kirker was absent from the legislature for one term. He was then elected to the house of representatives for the fifteenth and to the senate for the twentieth through the twenty-third general assemblies (1816-17, 1821-25), serving as speaker of the house in the fifteenth. It was while serving as speaker of the senate in the fifth general assembly that he became acting governor.

During Kirker's first year as acting governor the settlers in the western section of the state were alarmed by the threat of an Indian uprising. In order to provide for the security of the outlying settlements, in September 1807 Governor Kirker issued general orders calling up the first and second divisions of the Ohio militia. At the same time he sent Thomas Worthington and Duncan McArthur on a mission to

Greenville and other towns on the frontier to ascertain whether there was danger of an attack by the Indians. They reported that there was no indication of hostility on the part of the tribes and brought one of the chiefs to Chillicothe to convince Governor Kirker of their peaceful intentions. Kirker thereupon countermanded his orders mobilizing the militia.

In 1808 there were three candidates in the gubernatorial race: Kirker, Worthington, and Samuel Huntington, all nominally Democratic Republicans. The main issue in the contest was the question of judicial review of legislative acts. Huntington, who was chief justice of the state supreme court, favored the power of the courts to declare laws unconstitutional, while Worthington was the chief advocate of the supremacy of the legislature. Kirker held a position similar to Worthington's and divided the vote of those who opposed a strong court; Kirker and Worthington received 3,397 and 5,601 votes respectively to 7,293 for Huntington.

After his defeat Kirker returned to his duties as a legislator and to other public services. From January to October 1821 he was an associate judge of the court of common pleas in Adams County, and in 1824 he served as a presidential elector, casting his vote for Henry Clay. At the end of his career as a public servant he retired to his Liberty Township farm. His wife had died in 1824. He lived on until 1837, and upon his death was buried in the family burial plot on the farm.

Thomas Kirker rose from an uneducated Irish immigrant to a leading citizen of his adopted state largely by his own efforts. He possessed a fine physical appearance and was generally popular with his neighbors and colleagues. Although most historians agree that Kirker was not a brilliant statesman, he was conscientious and exercised good judgment in the execution of his public duties. He played an important part in the state's early history and served her honorably and well.

The Ohio Historical Society   S. WINIFRED SMITH

SAMUEL HUNTINGTON
1808 - 1810

The third governor of Ohio, Samuel Huntington, was born in Coventry, Connecticut, on October 4, 1765. His father was Joseph Huntington, a minister of liberal views and a descendant of Simon Huntington who emigrated from England in 1633. His maternal grandfather, Ebenezer Devotion, was also a minister, as were three of his paternal uncles. As a boy he was adopted by his uncle and namesake, Samuel Huntington, signer of the Declaration of Independence and governor of Connecticut (1786-96).

He attended Dartmouth College until the end of his junior year and then transferred to Yale, graduating in 1785 at the age of twenty. Upon graduation his uncle sent him abroad for a tour of Europe. After his return he studied law and was admitted to the bar in Connecticut in 1793. He practiced in that state until 1800. In that year he made a trip to the Ohio country on horseback, visiting the Western Reserve and the Ohio Valley as far south as Marietta.

Early in the summer of 1801 he brought his family to Youngstown

7

and soon thereafter settled in the village of Cleveland. His family at that time consisted of his wife—the former Hannah Huntington, a distant cousin whom he had married in 1791—two sons, Julius C. and Cobert, and Miss Margaret Cobb, a governess. In a letter to Moses Cleaveland he described the trip west as follows: "I have moved my Patriarchal Caravan through the wilderness to this Canaan. I was nine days on the Journey, with two Waggons, ten oxen, three horses, seven Cows and eighteen persons in my Retinue. We slept seven nights in the open air (after leaving the settlements in New York State)."

When Huntington arrived in Cleveland it was a village of a few log houses. One of them, a "pretentious," two-room, hewn log house, had been built for Huntington by Amos Spafford. It stood on the bluff south of Superior Street overlooking the present site of the Erie Railroad depot. It is related that one night in 1802 as Huntington was riding home through the swamp a mile or two from his home he was attacked by a pack of wolves. He fought them off with an umbrella, and with his horse running at top speed, reached home safely. Indians still roamed freely about the little settlement.

Huntington wrote Cleaveland in November 1801: "We have now here about 200 Indians going up the Cuyahoga. They have a jealousy of my coming here, owing to a story that has been propagated amongst them, that I am raising Soldiers to drive them out of the country. I have had a great number of Workmen here who they think are Soldiers in Disguise."

A different danger also threatened the settlers: the prevalence of malaria arising from the swamps. This last peril probably induced Huntington to move to Newburgh at the falls of Mill Creek where he bought the grist mill which had been operated by W. W. Williams for two or three years. In 1807 he traded three hundred acres in Cleveland for a large tract on the Grand River owned by John Walworth and moved to Painesville Township. There with two others in 1812 he founded the village of Fairport, where he erected the first warehouse in Lake County.

Soon after coming to Ohio, Huntington was filling positions of responsibility. Governor St. Clair appointed him lieutenant colonel of the Trumbull County militia in charge of the troops of the Western Reserve. In 1802 he was elected one of the supervisors of roads and in the same year was appointed justice of the peace and was given priority on the court of quarter sessions. He favored statehood and opposed the arbitrary rule of Governor St. Clair. He was elected as delegate to the Ohio Constitutional Convention in 1802, where he acted in harmony with the Chillicothe Junto.

He was elected to the senate of the first general assembly and was chosen speaker, but in April 1803 the general assembly selected Huntington as judge of the supreme court. His commission is said to be the first issued under the authority of the state. In 1804 he succeeded Return J. Meigs, Jr., as chief justice of the court. His most important decision while on the supreme bench was that rendered in the case of *Rutherford* v. *M'Faddon* in which he upheld the doctrine of judicial review of acts of the legislature with arguments comparable to those used by John Marshall of the United States Supreme Court. Calvin Pease, presiding judge in the circuit court in the eastern district, and George Tod, Huntington's associate on the supreme court, were both tried in impeachment proceedings for similar opinions. Huntington was spared trial, for in the meantime he had been elected governor.

The court question was the principal issue in the 1808 election, and Huntington, who had the support of the Federalists and the "Quids," or pro-court Republicans, defeated Worthington and Kirker, who split the anti-court Republican vote.

Huntington's administration was a stormy one. There was much excitement over the impeachment trials—both judges were acquitted by a single vote—and over Tiffin's "Sweeping Resolution," the principle of which was enacted into a law terminating the tenure of judges holding seven-year terms under the constitution (including interim appointees) in 1810. Another major concern was the threat of war with Great Britain, which would leave Ohio in a crucial position. There was much agitation also over the temporary location of the capital at Zanesville and the question of its permanent location. It was during this administration that Ohio's "Blue Laws" were passed, but there appears to be no evidence that Huntington, though a New Englander, had advocated them.

Governor Huntington was not a candidate for reelection but ran against Thomas Worthington for the United States Senate. He was defeated, however, and at the close of his term retired from public life and returned to his splendid estate near Painesville. In 1813 he was appointed army paymaster under General William Henry Harrison and with the general visited a fort at Cleveland named in Huntington's honor. He died on June 8, 1817, of injuries received while supervising repairs on the road from his estate to the Fairport harbor.

Samuel Huntington was a man of small stature but of abounding energy. He was well educated and his polished manners and command of the French language indicated that he may have spent some time in France. A natural leader, he was prominent in college life and eminent in the civil affairs of his adopted state. He was personally popular and numbered among his friends and correspondents such men as Gideon Granger, Arthur St. Clair, Jeremiah Morrow, Edward Tiffin, Thomas Worthington, and Elisha Tracy. The latter wrote him from Washington that he had not seen "one wry face" when it was mentioned that Huntington had been elected governor of Ohio. His business methods were efficient and ethical. As a lawyer and a public servant he was both able and honest, and his influence on the history of Ohio is significant. Perhaps his greatest contribution was his support of the doctrine of judicial review of legislative acts, now a generally accepted judicial principle.

The Ohio Historical Society   S. WINIFRED SMITH

RETURN J. MEIGS, JR.
1810 - 1814

The fourth governor of Ohio was Return Jonathan Meigs, Jr. He was of English ancestry, being a descendant of Vincent Meigs, who emigrated from Weymouth, England, to Weymouth, Massachusetts, about 1634. His father, Colonel Return Jonathan Meigs, won distinction during the Revolution at the battle of Sag Harbor. The latter was appointed a surveyor for the Ohio Company of Associates and arrived at Marietta in 1788 with the earliest immigrants.

R. J. Meigs, Jr., was born at Middletown, Connecticut, on November 17, 1764. Like his predecessor, Governor Huntington, he graduated from Yale in 1785, studied law, and was admitted to the Connecticut bar. In 1788 he married Sophia Wright and the same year followed his father to Marietta. There he practiced law, kept a store, engaged in farming, and served in numerous public offices.

When the first court was organized at Marietta in 1788, he was appointed clerk. In 1794 he was made the first postmaster at Marietta,

11

and in 1798 he was appointed a judge of the territorial court. The following year he was elected to the territorial legislature, and in 1803 he was appointed chief justice of the newly organized state supreme court. He resigned from the court in October of the same year he was appointed in order to accept appointment as commandant of the United States troops and militia in the St. Charles district of Louisiana Territory. The next year he was appointed a judge in Louisiana, but in 1807 he requested and received an appointment as judge in Michigan Territory. He resigned, however, before assuming the post to become a candidate for governor of Ohio.

He received a slight majority of the popular vote, but the general assembly declared him ineligible because of his residence outside the state during the four years preceding his election. The same legislature, however, appointed him to fill the vacancy in the United States Senate created by the resignation of John Smith. He was reelected to the senate for the next term but served only until May 1, 1810, when he resigned to run again for governor.

The issue of the campaign, as in 1808, was the power of the courts to declare legislative acts unconstitutional. Meigs, a conservative Republican, had the support of the Federalists and Quids and was elected. He was reelected for a second term in 1812 over Thomas Scott by a vote of 11,859 to 7,903. The result indicated an anti-Tammany trend in state politics.

It was during Meigs's first term that the general assembly located the permanent capital on the "high bank of the Scioto" opposite Franklinton and created a commission to plan for the construction of a statehouse and penitentiary. Meigs has the distinction of being the first governor on record to recommend the construction of a state prison. Although the power of the early governors of Ohio was strictly limited, Governor Meigs gave real leadership in the war of 1812 by recruiting 1,200 state militia in time for Hull's rendezvous at Dayton. At the time of Hull's surrender Meigs came in for severe criticism, but this was proved unjust and may have reacted in his favor in the 1812 campaign.

In recognition of his war services President Madison appointed him postmaster general in 1814 and he resigned the governorship. He served as postmaster general until forced to retire in 1823 because of ill health. The rapid growth of the postal system made its administration extremely difficult, and this gave rise to charges of mismanagement. Two congressional investigations were held, but the gravest charge which could be proved was inefficiency.

After resigning as postmaster general, Meigs returned to Marietta, where he died March 29, 1825. He is buried in Mound Cemetery, where his grave is marked by a monument bearing a long inscription reciting his public services and family devotion. He was survived by his wife and his only child, Mary.

Governor Meigs was striking in personal appearance. He was tall, erect, and well proportioned. He had a high forehead, an aquiline nose, and penetrating black eyes under dark arched brows. His expression was intelligent and benign in keeping with his character. In his various offices he proved himself a worthy public servant who made a notable contribution to the early history of his state and the nation. Fort Meigs and Meigs County, Ohio, were named in his honor.

The Ohio Historical Society   S. WINIFRED SMITH

OTHNIEL LOOKER
1814

Upon the resignation of Governor Meigs in March of 1814, Othniel Looker, speaker of the senate, became acting governor of Ohio under the provisions of the constitution of 1802. Comparatively little is known of his life. Sketches published in various places prior to 1920 are very incomplete and largely inaccurate. The following account is from the most reliable sources available.

Othniel Looker was born at Hanover, Morris County, New Jersey, on October 4, 1757. His ancestry could not be traced, but there are records of a family of that name at Elizabethtown, New Jersey, at least as early as 1686. A William Looker of that city was a deputy to the provincial council of New Jersey.

Othniel Looker enlisted at Elizabethtown in May 1776 in the New Jersey militia and served as private throughout the Revolutionary War. In 1779 he married Pamela Clark, a daughter of Abraham Clark of Elizabethtown, who was a member of the first vigilance committee in New Jersey, a member of the first Continental Congress, and a signer of the Declaration of Independence. About 1788 Looker moved to Vermont for about a year and then to New York state where he represented Saratoga County in the New York assembly in 1803 and 1804.

Having received a grant of land in the West for his war services, he came in 1804 to Hamilton County, Ohio. According to several accounts he settled in Harrison Township; the tax duplicate of Hamilton County for 1810 indicates, however, that he was paying taxes on 157 acres in Crosby Township, but there is no entry for that year in Harrison Township. He soon became widely known and respected, for he was elected to the Ohio House of Representatives in 1807 and thereafter represented Hamilton County in the house in the six, seventh, and eighth general assemblies (1807-9) and in the senate in the ninth, tenth, and twelfth through the fifteenth (1810-12, 1813-17). He was speaker of the senate in the 1813-14 assembly and thus became acting governor from March 25 to December 8, 1814, for the remainder of Governor Meigs's unexpired term. He discharged his duties with ability, but his brief tenure was uneventful. One incident, however, is worthy of note. In August 1814 he issued a call for five hundred volunteers to join an expedition under General Duncan McArthur against the Indians on lower Lake Michigan. He became a candidate for governor for the next term, but he lacked the prestige of his opponent, Thomas Worthington, and was defeated. Looker carried only five counties including his own, and polled only 6,171 votes to 15,879 for Worthington.

In 1816 Looker served as a presidential elector when the electors from Ohio voted for James Monroe and Daniel D. Tompkins. He remained in the senate until 1817 and then returned to Hamilton County, where in the same year he was made one of the associate judges of the court of common pleas, serving until 1824. He then retired to his farm in Harrison Township and apparently lived there until after his wife's death in 1841. He then lived for a time in Cincinnati with his son James Harvey Looker, the eldest of his nine children, who was one of the earliest newspaper publishers in Cincinnati.

In 1844 the former governor went to Palestine, Illinois, to live with his daughter Rachel, the wife of Judge Joseph Kitchell of that place. He became a highly respected member of the Illinois community. His last public address was made there on the Fourth of July, 1845, when, dressed in his continental uniform and overcome with emotion, he contrasted the early history of the country with its splendid destinies. He died within the month (July 23) and was buried in the Kitchell family lot. A monument was erected to his memory on the Looker farm in Harrison Township. Governor Looker had lived an honorable and useful life, and holds a record for longevity among former governors of the state. He has the distinction of being the only Ohio governor who served in the American Revolution.

The Ohio Historical Society   S. WINIFRED SMITH

THOMAS WORTHINGTON
1814 - 1818

Thomas Worthington, sixth governor of Ohio, was born at his father's estate near present Charles Town, West Virginia, in 1773. His Quaker grandfather, Robert Worthington, came to America in 1714, and after residing near Philadelphia until about 1730, settled in the northern Shenandoah Valley, then in Virginia. Thomas' father, also named Robert, was a prominent planter and influential citizen. His estate adjoined that of Samuel Washington, and George Washington had a farm nearby.

Left an orphan at seven, Thomas received little formal education. At eighteen he went to sea for two years and then returned to the modest estate he had inherited from his father in Berkeley County. He engaged in farming, stockraising, and surveying. In 1796 he made a trip to the Scioto country and determined to settle in the village, later named Chillicothe, then being laid out by his friend Nathaniel Massie. The next year he returned to Chillicothe with his brother-in-law Edward Tiffin, and each built a long cabin in the village. The following spring they brought their families and manumitted slaves and settled there.

17

Both Tiffin and Worthington rose rapidly to places of leadership in the new territory. Worthington was elected to the first and second territorial legislatures, where he served on important committees. A Republican, he worked against the administration of the Federalist Governor St. Clair and went to Washington to represent the opposition to the governor and to lobby for immediate statehood for the eastern section of the territory. His efforts were successful and he became an influential member of the constitutional convention of 1802.

Upon the organization of state government Worthington was elected to the house of representatives from Ross County, but was at once elected by the general assembly as one of the first two United States senators from Ohio. He served prominently in that body from 1803 to 1807 and again from 1811 to 1814. In the interim he was a member of the house in the sixth general assembly (1807-8). During his second term in congress he aroused much antagonism by opposing the entrance of the country into war with Great Britain, but vigorously supported the war after hostilities were begun.

In the fall of 1814 Worthington was a popular candidate for governor and was elected in October by an overwhelming majority over Othniel Looker. Inaugurated as governor on December 8, his first concern was the successful prosecution of the war. After peace came he encouraged a strong militia, advocated county poor farms, proposed state regulation of banks, and favored a public elementary school system. Worthington had little opposition for reelection in 1816 and won a decisive victory over James Dunlap and Ethan Allen Brown. During this term, 1816-18, the governor continued to press the measures advocated in his first inaugural and to urge penal reforms and encourage home manufacturing. It was at the beginning of Worthington's second term that the state capital was moved from Chillicothe to Columbus.

At the close of his administration Worthington retired from politics for a time and devoted his energies to his numerous business enterprises, which included farming, stockraising, milling, and river shipping. In 1821 he was elected to the general assembly from Ross County. In that year he lost by one vote election to the United States Senate to serve the remainder of William Trimble's unexpired term. Between 1821 and 1825 he served three terms in the state house of represenatives, where he exerted much influence in support of progressive legislation, including an elementary public-school law and the authorization of canal construction. He was a member of the important commission for locating and supervising the construction of canals.

He retired from politics after 1825 but continued his business activities in spite of failing health. He made several long trips in the interest of his business and in the hope of benefiting his health. On one of these he died in New York City, June 20, 1827. He was buried at Adena but was later moved to Grandview Cemetery, Chillicothe, where his grave is marked by a memorial stone.

Worthington was a man of many talents. He was an astute businessman, an honest statesman, and a capable leader. He was sincerely religious and his moral character was above reproach. He appreciated the beautiful in nature, in literature, and in architecture. Adena, his imposing mansion near Chillicothe, was noted for its refinement and hospitality. Its mistress and the mother of his ten children was the former Eleanor Swearingen, whom Worthington had married in Virginia in 1796.

The Ohio Historical Society   S. WINIFRED SMITH

ETHAN A. BROWN
1818 - 1822

Ohio's seventh governor, Ethan Allen Brown, was born at Greenwich, Connecticut, on Long Island Sound, on July 4, 1776. His father, Roger Brown, was a prosperous farmer and Revolutionary patriot. The youngest of seven children, Ethan in his early years helped out on the farm and studied under the supervision of an Irish tutor employed by his father. He was an apt pupil, becoming especially proficient in French, Latin, and Greek. At the age of twenty-one he went to New York, where he spent five years in Alexander Hamilton's law office.

After he passed the bar examination in 1802, Brown and a cousin rode horseback through Pennsylvania, then purchased two flatboats loaded with flour, which they floated down to New Orleans. Finding no market there, they took passage to Liverpool, England, where they sold the flour and returned to the United States. The following year Brown undertook another western journey, this time to select a tract of land in which his father wished to invest. He chose an attractive spot on the west bank of the Ohio River some thirty-five miles below

Cincinnati and purchased several thousand acres. A decade later the town of Rising Sun, Indiana, was laid out just south of the Brown estate, which came to be known as "Parterre."

In 1804 Brown moved to Cincinnati, where he was befriended by the noted pioneer Judge John Cleves Symmes. A man of varied talents, he performed in amateur theatricals and won respect as an orator. In addition, his professional activities led him into the field of politics. Though a native of Connecticut and one-time student of the nation's leading exponent of Federalism, he affiliated himself with the Republican party and soon rose to local prominence. Except for a term as prosecuting attorney of Hamilton County, the first position Brown held was a seat on the Ohio Supreme Court.

A bitter struggle between the proponents of legislative and judicial supremacy had resulted in a Pyrrhic victory for the latter. The legislature retaliated by passing the notorious "Sweeping Resolution," by which all of the supreme court posts as well a number of other state offices were declared vacant. The triumphant general assembly proceeded to appoint three judges, of whom Brown was one. His record as a jurist vindicated the choice, if not the events preceding it. While on the bench his character and conduct were unassailable, and he was rewarded with reelection in 1817.

In the previous year, although he had not declared himself a candidate for governor, Brown received more than 1,600 unsolicited votes in the election won by the incumbent, Thomas Worthington. In 1818, with the latter out of contention, Brown was elected governor by an overwhelming margin over James Dunlap of Chillicothe. He took the helm at the beginning of a period fraught with tragic overtones and set a course for the state which ultimately brought it again to comparatively placid waters. Ohio was engulfed in the economic depression of 1819, a year that saw many farms and businesses lost to their owners. Many westerners were convinced that the real villain was the United States Bank, especially after that institution announced that it would no longer accept state bank notes.

The scarcity of specie—gold and silver—spelled financial ruin for large numbers of Ohioans. The Ohio legislature responded by authorizing an annual tax of $50,000 on each of the bank's two branches in the state. With Governor Brown in complete accord, agents of the auditor invaded the Chillicothe branch in September 1819, and extorted from the protesting officials a sum in excess of $100,000 (the balance was later refunded). By this action Ohio defied a recent decision of the United States Supreme Court in which John Marshall denied the right of a state to tax an agency chartered by congress. The governor and most other prominent Ohioans felt the step justified on economic grounds, and this position was adopted by several other states. Legal steps taken by the bank finally brought the case before the supreme court at Washington in 1824. The attorneys included some of the ablest men of the day, among them Charles Hammond and John C. Wright for the defense, Henry Clay, William Wirt, and Daniel Webster for the bank. Ohio lost the case, and it is to her credit that the verdict was accepted gracefully.

Meanwhile, Governor Brown was bending his every effort toward lifting the state from the financial doldrums. From each county auditor he sought information concerning that county's manufactures, agricultural output, imports, and the like. Realizing that a full measure of prosperity could be attained only by rendering markets more accessible, he repeatedly advocated internal improvements, especially canals. He supplied the stimulus needed to induce the legislature to move in that direction. After several false starts, that body finally provided for exploratory surveys and named a canal commission, whose seven members included Brown, Worthington, and Alfred Kelley. The last-named, because of his vital role, has long vied with Brown for the title "Father of the Ohio Canals."

In 1820 Brown, opposed by Jeremiah Morrow and William Henry Harrison, was reelected in a convincing display of confidence. Midway through his second term he was the legislature's choice to succeed the deceased William Trimble in the United States Senate. There he continued to work for internal improvements in the capacity of chairman of the committee on roads and canals. His term expired in 1825, at which time Harrison captured his seat. Brown returned to Ohio and for the next five years served as one of three commissioners of the canal fund. He was primarily responsible for the negotiation of eastern loans with which the canals were financed. In this work his intimate friendship with Governor DeWitt Clinton, the guiding genius of New York's canal system, stood him in good stead.

Brown's active support of Andrew Jackson brought him in 1830 an appointment as chargé d'affaires to Brazil. His tour of duty lasted nearly four years at a critical period in Brazilian history, during which the reigning emperor was forced to abdicate. A less prudent man could have caused the United States much embarrassment, but Brown fulfilled his mission in a satisfactory manner. He returned from Brazil in 1834. In July of the following year he was appointed commissioner of the general land office at Washington, a post he occupied until October 1836, when, at the age of sixty, he retired to Rising Sun.

Here he busied himself with managing the family estate and caring for an elder brother and sister. His interest in politics did not slacken, however, and he served in the Indiana House of Representatives from 1841 to 1843. His life ended on February 24, 1852, while he was acting as vice president of the Democratic state convention at Indianapolis. He was buried at Rising Sun in the same plot with his father and six brothers and sisters. An appropriate tribute marks his grave.

Brown as an individual was cultured and intelligent; his wide circle of personal friends included Clinton, Jackson, Martin Van Buren, Lewis Cass, and others of the nation's great. Although he seems to have had ample opportunity to marry, and although Governor Clinton was determined to match him with a charming New York widow, Brown remained a bachelor throughout his seventy-six years.

The Ohio Historical Society   JOHN S. STILL

ALLEN TRIMBLE
1822, 1826 - 1830

Allen Trimble, Ohio's eighth and tenth governor, was born on November 24, 1783, in Augusta County, Virginia, of Scotch-Irish ancestry. His paternal grandfather, John Trimble, settled in Augusta County, where he was killed about 1763 by Indian raiders. James Trimble, Allen's father, fought at Point Pleasant and served with the Virginia militia during the Revolution, receiving for this service land warrants in Kentucky. He settled near Lexington late in 1784 when Allen was about a year old. As a young boy Allen received a sound education, but he was hindered by poor health from continuing his education beyond the age of seventeen.

Near the close of the century his father determined to manumit his slaves and settle in free territory north of the Ohio River.

In 1801 and again in 1803 Allen accompanied his father to Ohio to purchase land and to begin preparations for a home. The following year James Trimble died, and Allen, though not quite of age, assumed the responsibility for settling the estate and moving the family to the

24

new home, which was located in Highland County, about three miles from Hillsboro. For the next few years he was employed on the family farm and in surveying for nearby landowners. In 1808 he secured a position as county clerk of courts and recorder of deeds and moved to Hillsboro, which became his home for the rest of his life. During the War of 1812 he served as commander with the rank of colonel of an expedition against the Indians on the Eel and Wabash rivers. He also commanded a battalion of militia for a brief time before it was disbanded.

Thus coming into prominence in the county, Trimble was elected as a member of the Ohio House of Representatives in the fifteenth general assembly, 1816-17, the first session to meet in the permanent capital at Columbus. In 1817 he was elected to represent Highland and Fayette counties in the Ohio Senate, and was reelected for four consecutive two-year terms (1818-26) by substanial majorities. He was elected speaker of the senate in seven assemblies, proving his popularity as a presiding officer. He was acting governor from January 4, 1822, to December 28, 1822, for Governor Brown's unexpired term.

Trimble was a candidate for governor in the fall election of 1822 but lost to Jeremiah Morrow by a decisive vote (22,899 to 26,056). The third candidate, William W. Irwin, received only about half the vote for Trimble. At the next election for governor, when there was no third candidate, the vote was 39,526 for Morrow and 37,108 for Trimble. There were no outstanding issues as both candidates agreed on the main questions of the day: support of schools and internal improvements. The vote therefore represents the personal popularity of the candidates, and Trimble, a comparative newcomer, could not defeat the veteran statesman. By 1826, however, when Morrow was not in the running, Trimble won over three other candidates by an overwhelming majority. His work on the canal fund commission and as presiding officer of the senate had apparently increased his reputation and popularity. In 1828, as leader of the Clay Whigs, he again won the governorship over the Jackson party candidate. He did not seek the office for a third term.

As governor and legislator Trimble consistently supported progressive measures for education. In 1822 he appointed the commission headed by Caleb Atwater whose report formed the basis of Ohio's common school system. He urged state support of institutions of higher learning to keep western boys from going east for their advanced training. To him should go much of the credit for the state's notable progress in education in this early period. He contributed much also to the development of the state's canal system. In 1824 he was appointed as one of three members of the first canal fund commission to negotiate loans for financing their construction. During his first elected term as governor the general assembly authorized the executive to select a half million acres of land which the federal government had granted the state for subsidizing the canals. Trimble with an assistant personally examined lands in the Sandusky and Maumee river valleys for this purpose. Another vital question of the time was that of the increasing free Negro population in Ohio. Trimble favored the idea of African colonization of freed Negroes which might reduce the influx of free Negroes into the state, but little came of the scheme.

Although Trimble did not hold public office after 1830, he remained active in party politics, being a delegate to the National Republican convention in 1831 and a losing candidate for the legislature in 1832. His defeat is attributed to the increased strength of the Democratic party and the loss of control by the National Republicans. In 1855 he consented to become a candidate for governor on the American party ticket, apparently hoping to stem the tide of disunion.

After 1830 Trimble concentrated his energies on his agricultural interests. He was especially interested in improving domestic breeds of cattle and horses and was a stockholder in the Ohio Company for Importing English Cattle organized in Chillicothe in 1833. He was instrumental in establishing the state board of agriculture and became its first president (1846-48). He died in Hillsboro on February 3, 1870, at the age of eighty-six. He was survived by his wife, four sons, and a daughter.

The Ohio Historical Society   S. WINIFRED SMITH

JEREMIAH MORROW
1822 - 1826

The ninth governor of Ohio, Jeremiah Morrow, was born near Gettysburg, Pennsylvania, on October 6, 1771, of Scotch-Irish ancestry. His grandfather, Jeremiah Murray, a Covenanter from Londonderry, came to America about the middle of the eighteenth century and settled near Gettysburg, where the governor's father, John Murray, became a successful farmer. It was he who changed the family name to Morrow. Jeremiah spent his youth assisting on his father's farm and in securing a good education for the day, especially in mathematics.

At the age of twenty-three he caught the "Ohio fever" and started for the Ohio country in 1794, arriving the following spring in the Miami Valley. He settled first at Columbia, where he engaged in surveying, in farming, and in school teaching. A few years later he bought land in Deerfield Township, Warren County, made a clearing, and built a log house to which in 1799 he brought his bride, Mary Parkhill, a cousin from Pennsylvania.

Morrow's practical knowledge and sound judgment soon earned

the esteem of his neighbors, and they elected him to the second territorial legislature, which met in Chillicothe in 1801. In that body he acted in accord with the Chillicothe Junto in opposition to the administration of Governor St. Clair and in favor of immediate statehood. This was the first of many public offices to which he was appointed or elected over a period of more than forty years. He was elected delegate to the constitutional convention of 1802, in which he served as chairman of the committee on the qualifications of voters.

In January 1803 he was elected one of the four senators from Hamilton County in the first general assembly under the state constitution. Six months later he was elected from a list of seven candidates as Ohio's first congressman. He was reelected to this position with little or no opposition for four consecutive terms, thus serving in the house of representatives from 1803 to 1813, the entire period during which Ohio was entitled to but one representative. At the close of his fifth term in the house he was elevated to the United States Senate and served in that body until 1819.

Morrow was not a brilliant orator and his career in congress was not spectacular, but it was highly constructive. He was conscientious in the performance of his duties and excelled as a writer of reports. He was considered the outstanding authority on land policy, and as chairman of the committee on public lands while in both houses, drafted most of the legislation passed on that subject during his stay in congress. The land act of 1820, which decreased the minimum price of land to $1.25 per acre and permitted the sale of tracts as small as eighty acres, put into effect Morrow's policies.

Morrow declined reelection to the senate in 1819 and returned to his farm. He was not permitted, however, to remain long out of office, for in 1820 and again in 1822 he was appointed a canal commissioner. In the latter year he was elected governor over Allen Trimble and William W. Irwin, and reelected in 1824 when Trimble was his only opponent. The lack of differences in policies advocated by the candidates in both elections made the results an indication of Morrow's personal popularity.

When Morrow became governor, Ohio was still suffering from the business depression following the bank crisis of 1819. During his four years as state executive several factors contributed to a rising trend toward recovery. One of these was the beneficial effects of the federal land act of 1820, for which Morrow was directly responsible, and another was the stimulus to commerce created by the completion of the Erie Canal. More important still were the internal improvements within the state: the extension of the National Road into Ohio and the beginning of construction on the Ohio and Erie and the Miami canals. Morrow had been a strong advocate of internal improvements, and it seems fitting that he should have participated with Governor DeWitt Clinton in the ceremonies which opened both canal projects in July 1825.

Several important measures were passed by the general assembly during Morrow's administration. In addition to the act authorizing the construction of the canals, the session of 1824-25 passed two other very important measures which had the support of Governor Morrow. One was the law establishing a state-supported common school system and the other was the law drafted by Thomas Worthington for the evaluation and taxation of property which is substantially the basis for the state's present system.

At the close of his second term as governor Morrow declined to be a candidate for reelection but served in the state senate for the 1827-28 session and in the lower house in 1829-30 and 1835-36. His constituents in the fourth congressional district sent him again to congress in 1841. At the expiration of his term in 1843, just forty years after he first entered congress, he refused to be a candidate for reelection, stating that he felt out of harmony with the times. Only one of his colleagues in 1803, John Quincy Adams, was still in congress.

An active politician, Morrow was one of the founders of the Whig party in Ohio. He was president of the convention in December 1827 of a group which became the nucleus of the Whig party and presided at the Ohio Whig convention in Columbus in 1836. He was a delegate to the Republican national convention in Baltimore in 1831, and traveled East for the first time by stagecoach over roads which he had ridden many times on horseback. On three occasions he headed the ticket of presidential electors from Ohio.

Although Morrow had been showered with the highest honors in the gift of the people of his state, he was the most unassuming of men. After having been senator and governor, he did not disdain the humble offices of township trustee, school director, and supervisor of roads. His last years were spent among his books in an unpretentious home near Lebanon overlooking his saw and grist mill on the Little Miami River and a section of the Little Miami Railroad, of which he had served as first president. He died there in 1852 at the age of eighty and was buried in a country cemetery nearby. He was survived only by his eldest son, one of six children.

The Ohio Historical Society   S. WINIFRED SMITH

DUNCAN McARTHUR
1830 - 1832

Ohio's eleventh governor was Duncan McArthur. His parents, John and Margaret Campbell MacArthur (Governor McArthur spelled the name without the "a") were both descendants of proud Scottish Highland clans. John MacArthur emigrated to America sometime after 1746 and settled in Dutchess County, New York, where on January 14, 1772, his son Duncan was born. After the death of Duncan's mother when he was three, his father remarried and, in 1780, moved his family to western Pennsylvania. He was extremely poor, and Duncan, as the oldest of several children, had to work hard at home, and while still quite young was hired out on neighboring farms. This fact and the absence of schools on the frontier deprived the boy of formal schooling. He learned, however, to read and write by the age of twelve or thirteen.

As a youth his most exciting adventures were frequent crossings of the hazardous Allegheny trails with pack trains bringing supplies to the new settlements. At the age of eighteen he enrolled for service against the Indians and was in Harmar's disastrous campaign and other expeditions. During the winter of 1792 he was engaged as a salt boiler at Maysville, Kentucky. In the fall of that year he was employed by Nathaniel Massie as a chain carrier in a surveying tour into the Scioto Valley as far north as present Chillicothe, and thus became familiar with a region which he was later to help develop.

For the next two years McArthur was employed by the state of Kentucky as an Indian ranger to patrol the Ohio River. He was fitted for this occupation by physical courage, robust health, and fleetness of foot. In 1795 he was employed by Massie as an assistant surveyor, and early the next year assisted him in plotting the town of Chillicothe. In 1797 McArthur took his wife, the former Nancy McDonald, to his cabin near the newly established town.

Faced with the responsibility of providing for a growing family, McArthur began buying land for himself and locating land warrants for others. He was good judge of land and a shrewd buyer, so that by 1804 he had become one of the wealthiest landholders in the Scioto Valley and eventually was reputed to be one of the richest men in the state. In 1804-5 he built a fine mansion overlooking the Scioto Valley northwest of Chillicothe which came to be known as "Fruit Hill."

Duncan McArthur had a distinguished military career. In 1805 he was elected a colonel of the militia and three years later was commissioned a major general. He commanded one of the three militia regiments under General Hull in 1812. His troops were included in Hull's surrender, and he was placed on parole. Although McArthur had been elected congressman in 1812 by an almost unanimous vote, he preferred military duty and did not qualify when the time to take office came. On April 5, 1813, after his release from parole, he resigned from the militia and accepted a commission as a brigadier general in the regular army, serving under General Harrison in several important posts. After the latter's resignation in May 1814 McArthur was placed in command of the army in the Northwest.

Before and after the war McArthur was a member of several commissions for treating with the Indians. With Governor Lewis Cass of Michigan Territory he negotiated the Treaty of the Rapids of the Miami of Lake Erie (September 29, 1817), by which nearly all the remaining Indian lands in Ohio were ceded to the United States.

On the frontier, men of McArthur's prowess and business acumen were generally respected and often elected to places of public trust.

McArthur's first important public office was that of representative from Ross County in the Ohio General Assembly, to which he was elected in the fall of 1804. He served one term in the house (1804-5) and was elected in 1805 for the first of four consecutive two-year terms in the state senate (1805-13). He subsequently served in six more assemblies, three in the lower house (1815-16, 1817-18, 1826-27) and three in the upper chamber (1821-23, 1829-30), thus serving in a total of fifteen general assemblies. He was speaker in one session in the house (1817-18) and one in the senate (1809-10).

As a member of the general assembly McArthur varied from liberal to conservative. He acted with the liberal Republicans to impeach supreme court judges George Tod and Calvin Pease, but in opposition to the liberals voted for the removal of the capital to Columbus. He joined the Quid-Federalists in opposing the Tammany societies. A director of the United States Bank at Chillicothe, he bitterly opposed the act to impose a state tax on the branch banks, a course which made him very unpopular with the liberals. He was elected to congress in 1823 as an advocate of the federal bank. In congress he supported also Henry Clay's "American System" for internal improvements and a high tariff. He served one term without special distinction and was defeated for reelection in 1825.

In 1830, after resigning his seat in the state senate, McArthur became a candidate for governor on the National Republican ticket. In an indifferent contest he won over Robert Lucas by a narrow margin of 482 votes. (The vote was McArthur, 49,668; Lucas, 49,186; scattered, 226.) His administration was not marked by events of great importance, but progress was made in revising and recodifying old laws and in amending the tax laws to extend their coverage. Work on the canals progressed, the National Road was completed to Zanesville, and the assembly memorialized congress for another national road from Zanesville through Somerset, Lancaster, and Chillicothe to Maysville, Kentucky. Congress passed an act authorizing the road, but the bill was vetoed by President Jackson.

McArthur decided not to run in 1832 for a second term as governor. Instead, he became a candidate again for congress from the seventh district. He was defeated, however, by William Allen, the Jackson party candidate, who won the election by a single vote.

In December 1829, while serving his last term as state senator,

McArthur suffered an injury which impaired his health for the remainder of his life. After retirement from public life he was occupied with his agricultural and business interests, but his health failed rapidly and he died in Chillicothe on April 29, 1839. He was survived by five of his eleven children.

The Ohio Historical Society   S. WINIFRED SMITH

ROBERT LUCAS
1832 - 1836

Ohio's twelfth governor, Robert Lucas, was born at Shepherdstown, Virginia, on April 1, 1781. His mother was the former Susannah Barnes, whose brother Joseph Barnes experimented with steamboats many years before John Fitch and Robert Fulton. His father, William Lucas, though a descendant of Robert Lucas, an English Quaker who came to America in 1679, enlisted in the American Revolution and, in 1781, when the future governor was only a few months old, volunteered for service against the Indians on the frontier.

Little is known of Robert's early life, but he received part of his education from a Scotch tutor who taugh him mathematics and surveying. At the age of nineteen he moved with his family to near Portsmouth in present-day Scioto County, Ohio, then a part of the Northwest Territory. Three years later (1803) he was appointed surveyor of Scioto County, and with Nathaniel Beasley of Adams County, ran the line between the two counties.

At this time he joined the state militia, and up to the outbreak of hostilities with Great Britain in 1812, he held offices of increasing rank. During April and May 1812, as a brigadier general under Major General Duncan McArthur, he organized a battalion of volunteers from his brigade of Ohio militia. In General Hull's campaign against Canada in the summer of 1812, however, he served in several capacities, holding the rank of captain in the regular army as well as his position of brigadier general in the militia. Returning home after Hull's surrender, he found his wife very ill, and in October she died, leaving a daughter, then about a year and a half old.

In February 1813 he was appointed a lieutenant colonel in the regular army. Dissatisfied with an assignment, he resigned in June of the same year and again took up his duties with the militia, but he saw no further actual combat. In 1816 he was raised to the rank of major general and given command of the 2d militia division.

After the war Lucas turned his attention to politics. He had already served one term in the Ohio House of Representatives (1808-9), and in 1814 was elected to the state senate. He continued to represent his district, composed of Scioto and one or more neighboring counties, in the senate until 1822 and again in 1824-28 and 1829-30. He was returned to the lower house for the 1831-32 session, his last in the general assembly. As a lawmaker, Lucas actively supported legislation favoring the canals and the public school system. He consistently advocated also a strong militia.

In 1816, during his second term in the senate, Lucas married Miss Friendly Ashley Sumner and at about that time moved to Piketon in newly organized Pike County. He opened a large general store in his home on the main street of the village. In 1822-23, in an interval between tours of duty in the senate, he built one of the finest houses then in southern Ohio. "Friendly Grove," as he named the place in honor of his wife, is still standing on its original site two miles east of Piketon.

By 1830 his military and legislative service had made Lucas one of the most prominent men in the state. From 1825 on he had been an ardent supporter of Andrew Jackson. He was, therefore, a logical choice of the Democratic Republicans for governor and was unanimously nominated in the first state nominating convention in Ohio. The National Republicans announced through the newspapers the candidacy of Duncan McArthur, friend and war comrade of Lucas. A spirited campaign resulted in McArthur's election by a small majority.

For Lucas the sting of defeat was eased by reelection to the seat in the house of representatives which he had held in 1808-9. In May 1832 he had the signal honor of being elected temporary and permanent chairman of the first Democratic national convention.

Lucas was again the Jacksonian candidate for governor in 1832 and won the election over Darius Lyman, union candidate of the National Republicans and Anti-Masons, by a majority of over eight thousand votes in a contest fought mainly on the bank question. His inaugural address stressed encouragement to free public schools and the need for revision of the militia laws. His first term was largely uneventful, but he proved his ability as a competent executive and was reelected in 1834 for a second term over James Findlay, the anti-Jackson candidate.

It was during his second term that Lucas played such an energetic and decisive role in the "Toledo War." Both Ohio and the territory of Michigan claimed a strip of territory about five to eight miles wide along the northern border of Ohio within which lay the important lake port of Toledo, the probable terminus of the Miami-Erie Canal. In supporting Ohio's claim, Lucas called out the militia and led them to the border to face the forces of the acting governor of Michigan Territory, Stevens T. Mason. Only the intervention of President Jackson and his commissioners averted open war. Congress finally settled the question in Ohio's favor, but compensated Michigan with a large tract north and west of Lake Michigan.

Also during his second term, Lucas was appointed by President Jackson as a United States Commissioner to negotiate a treaty with the Wyandot Indians near Upper Sandusky. Lucas met with the Wyandots on their reservation in August, September, and October of 1834, but was unable to obtain their consent to a removal to the west and the cession of their lands to the United States. It was not until 1842 that the Wyandots finally agreed to such a treaty.

Governor Lucas protested the use of his name in 1836 as a candidate for a third term, but agreed to run for the United States Senate. He was defeated by William Allen and retired to Friendly Grove. Two years later President Van Buren appointed Lucas governor and superintendent of Indian affairs in the newly created territory of Iowa. Lucas was well qualified for the post, but his administration was embittered by the hostility of an ambitious secretary and the resentment of a legislature jealous of the governor's veto power. He was involved in another boundary dispute, this time between Iowa Territory and Missouri. He was replaced as territorial governor in 1841 and retired to his farm near Iowa City.

Again in Ohio in 1843, Lucas was induced to become the Democratic candidate for congressman in the eighth district. Defeated, he returned to Iowa City to reside for the rest of his life. He emerged from retirement to serve as a member of the convention which formed the state constitution of Iowa in 1844. In the same year he constructed a substanial two-story brick house at "Plum Grove." Here he spent his last years in the midst of his family, occupying much of his time in composing religious poems and hymns. He died on February 7, 1853, and was buried at Iowa City. He was survived by his wife and six children.

The Ohio Historical Society   S. WINIFRED SMITH

JOSEPH VANCE
1836 - 1838

In 1836 Robert Lucas was succeeded as governor of Ohio by Joseph Vance, who became the state's thirteenth executive. Vance was born in Catfish, now Washington, Pennsylvania, on March 21, 1786. His father, Joseph C. Vance, a Virginian whose Scotch-Irish forebears had emigrated to Virginia long before the Revolutionary War, had fought during the war under General Daniel Morgan, married in 1781, and not long after started West, dwelling for a time at several places along the way. About 1801 he moved into Ohio from May's Lick, Kentucky, finally settling on a farm two and a half miles north of Urbana.

Under pioneer conditions the son Joseph had very little opportunity for an education, a lack which he felt keenly throughout his career. As a boy of fifteen he proved his resourcefulness and courage by saving money from his wages as a wood cutter at the May's Lick salt works, buying a team of oxen, and peddling salt to the wilderness settlements. In 1805 he moved to Urbana with his father, who laid out the town that year, and two years later married Miss Mary Lemen of Urbana.

After his father's death in 1809 he took possession of the family farm, which became his home for the rest of his life.

Vance's first public office was that of secretary of the board of county commissioners, which paid a salary of forty dollars a year. At the age of twenty-three he organized an independent rifle company and was elected its captain. During the War of 1812 his company became part of the state militia, and thereafter Vance rose progressively from captain, major, and colonel to brigadier general.

Vance's qualities for leadership were soon evident to the voters of Champaign County, and in 1812 they elected him to the lower house of the eleventh general assembly. He was reelected to the twelfth, fourteenth, and eighteenth assemblies (1813-14, 1815-16, and 1819-20). In his first term he voted regularly for measures in support of the war. In the crucial bank question he supported the United States Bank against the state of Ohio.

In the fall of 1820 Vance was elected for the first of seven consecutive terms in the lower house of congress (1821-35). His chief interest in his legislative career was that of internal improvements in the West. He actively supported bills for the extension and repair of the Cumberland Road, for a road from the lower rapids of the Maumee to the western border of the Western Reserve, and for numerous canal projects. In 1824 he won his third term by an overwhelming vote of 4,342 to 16 for his opponent. From then on into the thirties he rarely had an opposing candidate in his district.

In his third term he was made chairman of the committee on military affairs and chairman of the board of visitors of the Military Academy at West Point. He also was instrumental in securing the passage of bills for granting subsidies to the Ohio and the Miami canals. Active in the antislavery movement in these years, Vance allied himself with John Quincy Adams in opposing the so-called Gag Resolution and in advocating the right of petition. He was defeated for reelection in 1834 in a close race with Samuel Mason.

In 1836 Vance accepted the nomination for governor and was elected in the first Whig victory in the state. As governor, Vance gave substanial support to the public school system, advocating that federal surplus funds be used for the schools, and he urged the completion of the canals then under construction. He favored the recharter of the United States Bank, and he urged the abolition of capital punishment.

Governor Vance was a forceful and capable executive, but he lost his popularity with the antislavery people of the state by the extradition of John B. Mahan, wanted in Kentucky for aiding the escape of two slaves. This action probably contributed more than any other one cause to his defeat for reelection in 1838, when he lost to the Democratic candidate, Wilson Shannon.

During Vance's administration there occurred an abortive rebellion in Canada in which a number of Ohioans, gathered in so-called Hunters', or Patriots', Lodges, attempted to take part. Though severely critical of their actions, Vance did not believe that he had any authority to interfere, though he promised the secretary of state and the army commander at Detroit to do all in his power to prevent the removal of arms belonging to the state militia.

Vance refused to be a candidate for governor in 1840, but his plans for retirement were upset by his reelection to the state senate from the tenth district for the 1839-41 sessions. Here he headed the committee on banking and currency. Two laws close to Vance's heart, providing increased support for schools and additional funds for canal construction, were passed during these sessions.

In 1842 the former governor was nominated on the Whig ticket for congressman from the tenth district and won over Samuel Mason, by whom he had been defeated eight years previously. He remained in Washington for two terms (1843-47) and was one of the most active members of the house of representatives. For three years chairman of the committee on claims, he was a strong advocate of governmental economy. He objected to the annexation of Texas and bitterly opposed the Mexican War as a war of aggression.

At the end of his second term he retired to his farm. Although he did not hold regular office again, he served as a delegate to the national Whig convention in Philadelphia in 1848 and as a representative of his district to the Ohio Constitutional Convention of 1850-51. He took a leading part in the debates and was chairman of the committee on public institutions. On his way home from attending sessions of the convention in Cincinnati in December 1850, he suffered a stroke of paralysis and was forced to give up his duties. He died at his home near Urbana on August 24, 1852.

The Ohio Historical Society   S. WINIFRED SMITH

WILSON SHANNON
1838 - 1840, 1842 - 1844

The principal issue in the Ohio gubernatorial election of 1838 was the question of banking and currency. Wilson Shannon, the anti-bank Democratic candidate, defeated the incumbent, Joseph Vance, and became the fourteenth governor of the state.

Wilson Shannon was born near Mount Olivet in what is now Warren Township, Belmont County, on February 24, 1802, and was, therefore, the first governor of Ohio to be born in the state. He was the youngest of the nine children of George and Jane Shannon, an Irish family who had emigrated from Virginia to the Ohio country in 1800. His father was frozen to death while on a winter hunting expedition when Wilson was not quite a year old. The responsibility of providing for a family of nine fell to the widow and the older sons, several of whom became prominent in law and politics. By hard work and strict economy, the family was able to purchase an eighty-acre farm two miles west of their original home.

As a boy Wilson helped his brothers on the farm and attended a one-room school in the district until he was eighteen. With the financial aid of two of his brothers, he apparently attended for a time both Ohio University at Athens and Franklin College at New Athens before transferring to Transylvania University at Lexington, Kentucky. He left the university before graduation to study law in the office of his brother George at Lexington. Soon returning to Belmont County, he completed his legal studies under David Jennings and Charles Hammond. Being admitted to the bar in 1830, he formed a partnership with Judge Kennon of St. Clairsville.

As a young lawyer Wilson Shannon became ambitious for political office. In 1832 he was the Democratic candidate for congress from his district and was defeated by only thirty-seven votes. The following year he was elected for the first of two consecutive terms as prosecuting attorney for Belmont County (1833-37).

During the period of the early thirties the economic situation in Ohio as well as in the nation at large was deteriorating, partly as a result of the wild speculation and over-expansion in the West. After the issuance of Jackson's "Specie Circular" the New York banks suspended specie payment on May 10, 1837, and the banks of Ohio were soon forced to take the same action. Questions relating to banking and currency became the chief issue between the two major parties.

The Whigs, representing wealth and social position, defended the banks; the Democrats blamed the banks and the over-circulation of bank notes for the financial crisis. Under these conditions both parties prepared for the election of 1838. The Whigs renominated Vance and the Democrats named Wilson Shannon, then relatively unknown beyond his own district. Shannon made an active campaign throughout the state, advocating a limited program of internal improvements evenly distributed over the state and extensive reform of the state's banking system. He won the election by a majority of 5,738 and was inaugurated on December 13, 1838.

The Democrats, having secured also a majority in both houses of the general assembly, were able to enact legislation carrying out the governor's program. One of the most important of these measures was the bank commissioner act of February 25, 1839, which limited the circulation of bank notes, required the closing of banks which defaulted in payments after a thirty-day period, and provided for three commissioners to examine and report on the condition of the banks. The same month saw the passage, with the governor's approval, of a fugitive slave act with more stringent provisions than those of the federal law.

In the October elections of 1839 the Democrats increased their majorities in both houses, and the Democratic press hailed this as an indication of popular approval of the financial measures advocated by Governor Shannon and enacted by the general assembly. In his annual message in December 1839 the governor recommended the completion of internal improvements then under construction in order to arrest the mounting state debt. He also urged the continuance of the banking system established by the act of February 25, 1839, a policy which lost him the backing of the Locofoco Democrats of Cincinnati, who favored more drastic controls on banking than those provided for by that law. The conservative faction, however, came to Shannon's support, and he was renominated by acclamation at the Democratic state convention in January 1840.

The state campaign of that year was largely eclipsed by the furor of the national contest between Harrison and Van Buren. The Whigs, successful in both races, elected Thomas Corwin governor of Ohio by a plurality of 15,691. The tables were turned, however, two years later when Shannon defeated Corwin for reelection, the principal issue being banking and currency as in the last two gubernatorial contests.

Shannon's second term (1842-44) was characterized by a further breach between the Democratic factions, due in part to the relaxing of the stringent Latham bank act passed on March 7, 1842, and to the governor's support of Lewis Cass for the presidency.

In April 1844, Shannon resigned as governor to accept an appointment by President Tyler as minister to Mexico. While he held the office, relations between Mexico and the United States became severely strained over the annexation of Texas, and Shannon, tactless in his communications with the Mexican government, was recalled by Calhoun in March 1845 on the eve of the Mexican War.

Returning to Ohio from Mexico, the former governor engaged in the practice of law at St. Clairsville and Cincinnati until 1849 when he led a band of "Forty-Niners" to the California gold fields. On his return to Ohio two years later he again entered politics and was elected to the thirty-third congress (1853-55) from the district composed of

Belmont, Guernsey, Noble, and Monroe counties. He was a member of the committee on foreign affairs, but did not become prominent. He voted with three other Ohio Democrats for the Kansas-Nebraska bill, which precipitated a struggle between the free-state and proslavery forces in Kansas.

Shannon was destined to cope with the war in Kansas, for in 1855 President Pierce appointed him governor of Kansas Territory. Although personally in sympathy with the proslavery forces, he attempted to serve as peacemaker between the two factions. Successful in one or two instances, he eventually failed and war broke out. He was removed as territorial governor on August 21, 1856, and retired from public life. He returned to Ohio for only brief visits, maintaining his home and practice of law in Kansas until his death on August 30, 1877. Shannon was said to be a very fine looking man, six and a half feet tall and "straight as a pole." He was twice married and had eight children, several of whom survived him.

The Ohio Historical Society   S. WINIFRED SMITH

THOMAS CORWIN
1840 - 1842

Never in the history of American politics has there been such a riotous, rollicking campaign as that of 1840, when the Democrats were "sung and stung to death" by a fanfaronade of Whig oratory, spectacular parades, and noisy songs. In critical Ohio the chief campaign orator was Tom Corwin, "The Wagon Boy," nominated unanimously for governor by what was alleged to have been the largest convention ever held. Corwin not only won his own race but, acknowledged the official Democratic historian, "was the most powerful factor in General Harrison's campaign for President."

In 1840 Thomas Corwin was no newcomer to Buckeye politics. Although born in Bourbon County, Kentucky, July 29, 1794, he had lived in Lebanon, Ohio, since he was four. And he had politics with his meals as he listened to his father, Matthias, who served eleven terms in the Ohio House of Representatives, two as speaker. Young Tom's political career began as Warren County prosecuting attorney, 1818-28, and state legislator, 1821-23, 1829-30. In the next decade, when the

Whigs produced only minority reports, he served five terms in congress. There his talent for sharp satire and witty debate made him, said one contemporary journalist, "the terror of the House." With a national reputation as a Whig spokesman by 1840, Corwin had joined the Harrison movement; and he had earned considerable nonpartisan support at home by congressional speeches on two popular issues, the Michigan boundary dispute and the Cumberland Road extension.

Although the Whigs promised only what Corwin called "great *amendments* in the administration of public affairs," it was enough to upset Wilson Shannon, the incumbent governor, who ran under the handicap of hard times. James Buchanan wrote President Van Buren from Ohio that "it would seem that the whole population have abandoned their ordinary business for the purpose of electioneering"; and Corwin later claimed, "I have made more than *one hundred* regular *orations* to the people this summer. . . . I have, *first & last,* addressed at least seven hundred thousand people, men, women, children, dogs, negroes & Democrats inclusive." However accurate this estimate may have been, Corwin did speak in almost every section of the state, winning the acclaim of even conservative critics, who called him "the most famous stump speaker of his time."

The Jeffersonians who wrote the Ohio constitution warily permitted the governor few executive powers, and Corwin laughingly described as his principal duties, "to appoint notaries public and pardon convicts in the penitentiary." Nevertheless, he enthusiastically sponsored a Whig prescription for the sickness resulting from the Panic of 1837: establishing a state bank, and rechartering the safest of existing banks, but with joint liability of all for the debts of any one, and restrictions upon their circulation and profits. The Democrats still ruled the upper house, however, and Corwin's proposals were defeated in a crisis of inaction. As more banks failed and currency circulation contracted, Whig prestige shrank, and in 1841 the Democrats gained control of both houses and promptly enacted their own banking laws. Corwin, meanwhile, as one of the few lawyers outside the farmer-governor tradition, continued a sizable practice to supplement his $1,500 salary.

In 1842 Corwin foresaw an unfavorable season for Whiggery and declined to seek reelection; but when the convention nominated him by acclamation, he went unwillingly into the race. Since his party had never controlled the legislature, Corwin had to run not on the record but on promises. This weakness, plus the growing defection of antislavery Whigs to the Liberty party, let the "outs" back in by fewer than 4,000 votes, and the Wagon Boy suffered his only defeat in thirty-seven years of officeholding.

Though their national ticket was defeated in 1844, the Whigs carried Ohio, and Corwin was sent to the United States Senate. Here he was a powerful figure until his resignation in 1850 to become Fillmore's secretary of the treasury. Most notably, though he was not an "ultra" abolitionist, Corwin led the Whig opposition to the Mexican War, and gained popular support among many Whigs, peace-lovers, and antislavery men, who hoped he would be their presidential candidate in 1848. Rather than risk a party split, Corwin refused to lead these forces, and in a triumph of epaulettes, General Zachary Taylor was nominated. Again Corwin "ate and slept on the stump" throughout the successful campaign.

In 1853 Corwin retired from politics, returned to Lebanon, and resumed his lucrative law practice. Five years later, when the Republicans needed the popular orator, he was elected to congress from the seventh district, and reelected in 1860, after campaigning strenuously for Lincoln in a dozen states. In a final act of Whiggery, Corwin sought a compromise in the house committee of thirty-three, of which he was chairman. On the eve of Lincoln's inaugural, congress adopted the "Corwin Amendment," which would have made unconstitutional any interference with slavery where it existed. But it was too late; even Corwin admitted that "on both sides they are like bull-dogs eager for the fray."

To Lincoln the post of minister to Mexico was "perhaps the most interesting and important one within the whole circle of our international relations," and Corwin, regarded as a friend by Mexicans since his polemics against the war in 1847, was a logical choice. He filled the post capably, besting the confederacy's Colonel John Pickett in the diplomatic duel which kept the prize of Mexico's friendship for the North during the war.

Tom Corwin, who lived until December 18, 1865, once facetiously proposed that his tombstone read: "Dearly beloved by his family; universally despised by Democrats; useful in life only to knaves and pretended friends." Except for the reference to Sarah Ross Corwin and their five children, Corwin was unfair to himself. It was true that throughout his career Democratic editors and campaigners singled Corwin out for their bitterest attacks, but this was not because they despised him. Rather it was evidence of their respect for one of the most effective stump speakers in the nation: that crusty old critic, John Quincy Adams, ranked Corwin among the leading Whig orators of his day; Rutherford B. Hayes heard him "far excelling anything that [Edward] Everett did"; Chauncey Depew remembered him as "probably the most brilliant speaker of the period immediately preceding the Civil War"; and Robert Ingersoll crowned him "king of the stump."

Stocky, swarthy, and physically dynamic, Tom Corwin was an impressive figure on the platform, and his skill in argument, combined with a keen wit, made him a leading spokesman for Whig doctrine: support the Union at all costs, oppose divisive movements, and compromise when necessary. When the Whig party could no longer sustain its strategy, Corwin gave his support, and his eloquence, to the Republicans. In one of the critical periods of American history, Ohio's Tom Corwin played a leading role.

University of Virginia   J. JEFFERY AUER

THOMAS W. BARTLEY
1844

Upon the resignation of Governor Shannon the Democratic speaker of the senate, Thomas Welles Bartley, became acting governor of Ohio on April 15, 1844, and served until the close of the term in December of the same year. At that time he was succeeded as governor by his father, Mordecai Bartley, a succession which is unique in Ohio and at least rare in the history of state governments.

In 1809 Mordecai Bartley came from Fayette County, Pennsylvania, to Jefferson County, Ohio, where Thomas was born on February 11, 1812. At the close of the War of 1812 Bartley settled his family near Mansfield on a small farm which he bought and cleared. Here Thomas spent his boyhood helping on the farm, attending school, and imbibing politics, for when he was twelve his father began the first of four consecutive terms in congress.

At seventeen Thomas was graduated from Jefferson College, Canonsburg, Pennsylvania, and four years later, after having studied law at Mansfield and Washington, D. C., he was admitted to the Ohio bar and began practice at Mansfield. A few years later he was elected prosecuting attorney for Richland County and served two terms. This was the beginning of his rapid rise in a legal and political career. In 1839 he was elected for the first of two terms in the Ohio House of Representatives (1839-41). His service in the house was followed by two consecutive two-year terms (1841-45) in the state senate. During his legislative career he was a member of the important standing committee on the judiciary in both houses.

In 1843 he was elected speaker of the senate and thus came into the office of acting governor from April 15 to December 3, 1844. The general assembly had adjourned a month before Shannon's resignation, so that Bartley had little opportunity to function as governor. He did, however, present an annual message to the assembly on the same day that his father was inducted into office. A strong Van Buren man and a leader of the antibank Democrats, the younger Bartley had lost the nomination for governor at the Democratic state convention to David Tod by a single vote, and thus narrowly escaped opposing his father, the Whig candidate for the office of governor, in the campaign of 1844. He did not participate actively in the campaign, and the cordial relationship between father and son was not disrupted by their divergence in politics.

After his tour of duty in the senate Bartley served during President Polk's administration (1845-49) as United States District Attorney for the Northern District of Ohio, an appointment secured through the influence of Senator William Allen. Elected one of the first judges of the state supreme court under the new constitution, he served on the bench from February 1852 to February 1859, being chief justice for three years. His colleagues included such eminent jurists as Rufus P. Ranney, Jacob R. Swan, Allen G. Thurman, and Jacob Brinkerhoff.

After his retirement from the bench he practiced law in Mansfield, Cincinnati, and Washington, D. C., until his death on June 20, 1885. He was buried in Washington beside his second wife, Susan Sherman, a sister of Senator John Sherman and General William Tecumseh Sherman. He was survived by his third wife and a number of children.

A man of decided convictions vigorously defended, Bartley made many antagonists. In 1869 he wrote a would-be biographer that because of the "malevolence of the political & personal enemies" which he had made, he did not think justice could be done him while he lived. His most distinguished service to Ohio was that of judge of the supreme court. He wrote the opinion in the Toledo Bank case and concurred in the majority opinion in the Piqua Bank case, both of which involved the right of the state to tax chartered institutions. When the latter opinion was reversed by the United States Supreme Court, Bartley wrote a dissenting opinion on the mandate of the higher court, in which he denied that court the right of appellate jurisdiction over the state courts. In spite of his patriotism and ability he failed to see that such a policy could lead to disunion.

The Ohio Historical Society S. WINIFRED SMITH

MORDECAI BARTLEY
1844-1846

Mordecai Bartley, eighteenth governor of Ohio, was inducted into office on December 3, 1844, to succeed his son, Acting Governor Thomas Welles Bartley.

The Bartleys' English forebears settled in Loudoun County, Virginia, in 1724, whence Mordecai's father, Elijah, moved to Fayette County, Pennsylvania, where Mordecai was born on December 16, 1783. As a lad he attended district school between seasons of hard work on the farm. Married at the age of twenty-one to Elizabeth Welles, he moved to Jefferson County, Ohio, in 1809. During the War of 1812 he organized a company of volunteers and was elected their captain. He later was made adjutant of a regiment under General William Henry Harrison. After the close of the war Bartley selected a site for a home west of Mansfield in Richland County, a little in advance of the line of settlement.

A successful farmer, he engaged also in merchandising in Mansfield, whither he moved in 1834. In the meantime he had been elected to

represent Licking, Knox, and Richland counties in the Ohio Senate
(1816-18). In 1818 the assembly appointed him register of the Virginia
Military District school lands with office at Mansfield. This position
gave him an abiding interest in the public schools. He resigned the
office in 1823 to take a seat in the lower house of congress, which he
held four terms (1823-31). In his first congressional campaign he was
opposed by the able and energetic Alfred Kelley, but so great was
Bartley's popularity in his home town that his own vote was said to be
the only one cast for Kelley at Mansfield. Two years later he again
defeated Kelley, and in the two subsequent elections won over Eleutheros
Cooke.

While in congress Bartley did not often take part in the debates,
but he was alert to the interests of his district, which comprised a large
part of northern Ohio, including Sandusky and Cleveland. He was the
first to propose to congress a land grant to Ohio for the benefit of the
common school fund and was instrumental in securing a federal grant
for the improvement of several Lake Erie harbors. In the presidential
election of 1824, which was decided in the house of representatives,
Bartley, although an ardent supporter of Henry Clay, voted with the
Ohio delegation for John Quincy Adams. Declining renomination for
a fifth term, he supported Cooke as his successor in congress.

Upon retiring from congress Bartley resumed his agricultural and
mercantile pursuits at Mansfield. In 1844 he was nominated for governor
at the second of two Whig state conventions, after David Spangler of
Coshocton, who had been nominated at the first, declined to run. The
Democrats nominated David Tod. Although the state campaign was
somewhat confused by the presidential campaign of that year, in which
the question of the annexation of Texas and Oregon predominated, the
matter of the state banking system was again paramount in Ohio.
Tod's position was unsatisfactory to both the anti-bank radicals and
the conservative Democrats. This and other factors contributed to
Bartley's election by a small majority. The Whigs were successful also
in returning a plurality for Henry Clay in the presidential race and in
securing control of both houses of the general assembly.

The Whigs proceeded at once to carry out their state banking
program. A bill sponsored by Alfred Kelley was enacted into law on
February 24, 1845. Known as the Kelley Bank Act, it repealed the
earlier Latham and Bartley acts and remained the basic banking act

of the state for the next two decades. The statute provided for independent banks as well as a state bank which should be organized when seven branches had been established; it imposed upon stockholders a limited collective liability (instead of the full individual liability advocated by the Democrats), and it placed certain restrictions upon the issuance of bank notes. In his message to the legislature in December 1845, Governor Bartley declared that the effect of the law had been to restore confidence and contribute to the "rising prosperity of the State."

Another important financial measure of his administration was the Kelley Revenue Act of March 2, 1846, which equalized taxation and placed several classes of property, formerly exempt, upon the tax duplicate.

The conflict with Mexico which broke out in the spring of 1846 placed Bartley in a difficult position. Although the Ohio governor was opposed to the war, he felt it his duty to comply with President Polk's request for troops, and personally supervised the organization of Ohio's quota. In reference to the war he declared to the assembly: "If it be the object of our people to extend the influence of free institutions to other nations of the world, far more can be done by the moral influence of example, than by the conquest and force of arms."

The governor was involved also in a controversy with the governor of Virginia over the enforcement of the fugitive slave law. His position on the slavery issue is indicated by the fact that in his annual message to the general assembly in December 1845 and again in 1846 he advocated the repeal of Ohio's "Black Laws," which placed restrictions upon the free Negroes in the state, denying them the right to testify in the courts against a white man and requiring bond of them against their becoming public charges.

Bartley declined renomination for a second term and retired from public life to his home and business interests at Mansfield, where he lived out his eighty-seven years until his death on October 10, 1870.

Mordecai Bartley came into Ohio six years after its admission to the Union. He saw the population of the state grow from about 230,000 to over 2,500,000. The agricultural progress during this period is demonstrated by the fact that the farm which he hewed from the wilderness was, shortly before his death, the scene of a state-wide trial of mowers and reapers. A modest and unassuming man of high principle, his own statement of purpose and estimate of his career is found in his last message to the assembly: "In the humble part which I have taken in the public affairs of the State, I have been directed by an earnest desire to subserve the welfare of the people."

The Ohio Historical Society   S. WINIFRED SMITH

WILLIAM BEBB
1846 - 1849

Ohio's nineteenth governor was William Bebb of Butler County, the third native Ohioan to be elected to the office. His father, Edward, who had emigrated to America from Wales in 1795, was the first settler in the Welsh settlement of Paddy's Run, the present town of Shandon. Having built a two-story log cabin on land purchased on the Dry Fork of the Whitewater in 1801, he went east to Philadelphia and returned with his bride, a widow, the former Margaret Roberts Owens. William, the first of their three children, who was born on December 8, 1802, is said to have been the first white child born in Butler County west of the Great Miami River.

Before he was old enough to attend school, William received instruction in both English and Welsh from his mother. Probably from the age of seven or eight he received several months' schooling each year in the district school. One of his later teachers was David Lloyd, a well educated Welshman. When about twenty young Bebb began teaching. Accounts differ as to his first school, but they agree that he taught for a time at North Bend, the home of William Henry Harrison. At all events, he was married in 1824 to Sarah Shuck, who was also a teacher there.

In 1826 the Paddy's Run school was organized under the new state law, a new building was erected, and William Bebb was employed as the first teacher. Two years later Bebb and his wife opened a boarding school in a frame building erected for the purpose on the farm of Edward Bebb. The "Sycamore Grove School" was successful from the start, having from thirty to forty boys between ten and fourteen years old from Cincinnati and the South and a few local day pupils. One writer claims that Bebb's methods were similar to modern educational procedures. A number of his pupils became prominent. They included a later governor, William Dennison, and several eminent attorneys.

While conducting the school Bebb also studied law and in December 1831 passed the state bar examination. The following year he closed his school and began the practice of law in Hamilton, first in the office of his mentor, John Woods. From 1834 to 1840 he was the junior partner of John M. Millikin.

As a young lawyer Bebb became an active Whig politician. His first major effort was in the "hard cider" campaign of 1840 when he stumped the state for Harrison and Tyler. Four years later he was a delegate to the Baltimore convention which nominated Henry Clay for the presidency. Bebb was nominated for governor by the Whig party in 1846. The questions of banking and currency and taxation were again major issues, with Bebb favoring the continuation of the Kelley laws with only slight amendments. The campaign slogan was "Wm. Bebb and a Home Currency against David Tod and Pot Metal."

In his campaign over the state Bebb advocated also the repeal of the testimony clause of the Black Laws (and in the Western Reserve, the repeal of all these laws). The Democrats made capital of his favoring "Negro equality," especially in central and southern Ohio, indicating a growing sectionalism in Ohio politics. The Whigs won the contest, with Bebb receiving 118,869 votes to 116,484 for David Tod, the Democratic candidate. The Liberty party polled 10,797 for Samuel Lewis. The Whigs elected a majority of eight in the house of representatives, but the parties were tied in the senate.

Governor Bebb was inaugurated on December 12, 1846. The Mexican War was in progress and the Whigs in the general assembly passed a resolution condemning the war and President Polk. The governor was ardently opposed to the war, but like his predecessor honored the president's call for Ohio troops. Although his party had only a slight majority, Governor Bebb stated in his message to the general assembly at the close of his administration (January 5, 1849) that all but one of his principal recommendations had been adopted. The currency and revenue laws had been maintained with only minor revisions, the support of schools and colleges continued, and the state debt greatly reduced by strict economy and the increased sale of canal lands; monopolies had been curbed, conditions in the penitentiary had been ameliorated, and the construction of the new statehouse had progressed rapidly. The one exception was the repeal of the Black Laws, which he again strongly urged.

He took the occasion to express his views on numerous state and national problems. He recommended the calling of a constitutional convention and a revision of the constitution to provide for the election of all executive, legislative, and judicial officials directly by the people; to place a constitutional limitation on the state debt; to provide for biennial instead of annual sessions of the general assembly in order to reduce government expenditures; and to make improvements in the judicial system. On the national level he advocated the extension of the antislavery article of the Ordinance of 1787 to New Mexico and California and other territories which might be acquired.

Governor Bebb's term expired in December 1848, but his administration was continued until January 22, 1849, because of a delay in organizing the two houses of the assembly and in qualifying his successor. He had not been a candidate for reelection and did not again hold an elective office. He retained his interest in politics, however, and subsequently served as elector-at-large from Illinois on the Scott ticket. During Lincoln's administration he was appointed an examiner in the pension office at Washington and later (1868) declined an appointment as consul at Tangier, Morocco.

After retiring from the governorship, Bebb and his family moved to a farm of five thousand acres which he had purchased in a beautiful location on the Rocky River near Rockford, Illinois. Here occurred a tragic incident in which Bebb shot and killed one of a group of rowdies who came to serenade the home on the occasion of the marriage of one of his sons. He was tried in the Rockford County court for manslaughter but was acquitted. His attorneys were assisted by Thomas Corwin and W. T. Johnson, his friends from Ohio.

During the middle 1850's Governor Bebb visited Europe and Wales. While in Wales he encouraged a colony of Welsh to locate in eastern Tennessee. In 1860 he took his family to reside at Knoxville so that he could superintend the affairs of the settlement. The threat of war scattered the settlers and Bebb was warned not to return to Tennessee from Illinois, where he was speaking for Lincoln. His last years were spent at Rockford, where he died on October 23, 1873. His wife and three children survived. A son Michael was a noted botanist.

The Ohio Historical Society   S. WINIFRED SMITH

SEABURY FORD
1849 - 1850

Seabury Ford, the twentieth governor of Ohio, was born in Cheshire, New Haven County, Connecticut, on October 15, 1801. He was descended, in the sixth generation, from Timothy Ford, who had emigrated from Devonshire in England to Charlestown, Massachusetts, in 1637, and who afterwards became one of the original proprietors of the New Haven Colony. Seabury Ford was the fifth of seven children born to John and Esther Cook Ford.

John Ford acquired a large holding on the Western Reserve in 1804, and in 1807 he moved his family to Burton in Geauga County. Seabury Ford prepared for college at the Burton Academy, and returned to New Haven in 1821 to enter Yale. After graduation in 1825, he went back to Ohio to study law in the office of his uncle, Peter Hitchcock, and in 1827 was admitted to the bar. The next year he married his cousin, Harriet Cook. Five sons were born to them. While practicing law in Burton, Ford interested himself in the military affairs of Ohio, and he became a major general in the state militia.

61

Ford joined the new Whig party when it was organized in 1834, and the next year he was elected to the lower house of the thirty-fourth general assembly. Thereafter Ford was elected, either as a senator or a representative, to every general assembly through the forty-fifth, with the exception of the forty-second. He was speaker of the house in the thirty-ninth general assembly, and speaker of the senate in the forty-fourth.

In an age of oratory Ford was hampered by a distaste for public speaking, and once confessed to a friend that "nothing but the force of circumstances could drive me to it." In the Ohio legislature he became an expert upon tax and banking legislation. Perhaps Ford's most notable achievement as a legislator came in the repeal of the Loan Law of 1837.

The Loan Law was popularly known as the "Plunder Act," due to facilities it offered for raiding the state treasury. The law permitted the state of Ohio to loan money to railroads, and to subscribe to the stock of canal and turnpike companies. Ford pushed the repeal through the general assembly in 1840. A modern student has noted that the repeal of the Loan Law marked the beginning of a "general trend away from State ownership of, or participation in, internal improvements" as well as the start of a movement "towards laissez faire" in the relations between the state of Ohio and business organizations.

Like all the Whigs of the Western Reserve, Ford was strongly opposed to slavery, but fear of civil war prevented him from becoming a radical abolitionist. In 1838 he was defeated by Joshua R. Giddings in a very close contest for the Whig nomination for congress. Ford was an admirer of Henry Clay, and campaigned vigorously for the Kentuckian in the presidential election of 1844.

In January 1848 the Whigs nominated Ford for governor. The Mexican War, which the Whigs had opposed, had not yet concluded, and the Democrats nominated John B. Weller, who had served as a lieutenant colonel in Mexico. As a member of congress Weller had voted for the gag rule, and he was thought to be a southern sympathizer. The Ohio Whigs demanded that the Mexican War be ended, opposed any forcible annexation of Mexican territory, and insisted that if any territory was acquired otherwise, slavery should be excluded therefrom. "John B. Weller and war—Seabury Ford and peace!" became a Whig slogan.

The Whig campaign in Ohio was sadly embarrassed when, in

June, the national party nominated for president General Zachary Taylor, a southern slave owner. Salmon P. Chase at once issued his call for the Free Soil convention. The Free Soil secession had a disastrous effect on the antislavery voters of the Western Reserve, which had long been an impregnable Whig stronghold. Ford was desperately anxious to hold his party together, and he decided that he could best accomplish this by ignoring Taylor's candidacy. This naturally exposed him to the taunts of the Democrats, but in the outcome Ford was elected governor and Taylor was beaten in Ohio. During the campaign Ford vigorously urged the repeal of the Black Laws.

The election was the closest in the history of Ohio, and the only one which had to be decided by the legislature. The general assembly elected in 1848 was evenly divided between Whigs and Democrats, with the Free Soilers holding the balance of power. The forty-seventh general assembly convened on December 4, 1848, and its sessions were among the most turbulent on record. Ford was to have been inaugurated in December, but the event was delayed six weeks while the legislature struggled to organize itself. Ultimately, and after prolonged examination of the returns, the general assembly on January 22, 1849, decided that Ford had received 148,756 votes to 148,445 for Weller, a margin of victory of only 311 votes. Moved by the violence of the legislative sessions, Ford spoke feelingly in his inaugural address on the preservation of the Union and the fatal consequences which would follow its dissolution.

With the legislature so badly divided, little could be accomplished. However, the Black Laws, which discriminated against Negroes, were repealed. The question of a constitutional convention was submitted to the voters, and approved by them in the fall election of 1849. The forty-eighth general assembly then passed the necessary legislation and the convention met in the house of representatives on May 6, 1850. The constitution there adopted is still the basic law of Ohio. When Thomas Corwin resigned from the United States Senate to enter Fillmore's cabinet in July 1850, Ford appointed Thomas Ewing to succeed him.

Cholera struck Columbus in 1849, producing a panic in the city. Ford remained at the capital, and was confronted with a serious crisis at the Ohio Penitentiary, where the epidemic had created a chaotic situation. Ford granted pardons to the deserving, and restored order in the prison by a personal appeal in which he promised additional pardons to those who would keep their heads and aid in nursing the sick until the epidemic had run its course.

Ford's term as governor ended on December 12, 1850. On the first Sunday after his return to his home in Burton he suffered a paralytic stroke, from which he made only a partial recovery. The left side of his body was paralyzed, and he died in Burton, at the age of fifty-three, on May 8, 1855.

Ford was the last Whig governor of Ohio. He believed that the party of compromise alone was capable of achieving a peaceful solution of the slavery controversy, and almost to the end he appears to have cherished the hope that the Whigs could somehow be reunited and return to power.

Toledo Blade   HARVEY S. FORD

REUBEN WOOD
1850 - 1853

In the election year of 1850 the Whig party in Ohio was embarrassed by President Fillmore's failure to continue President Taylor's antislavery policy and by his support of the Clay compromise of that year. The Democrats, at first, likewise attempted to evade the slavery question; they nominated Reuben Wood, however, who was from the Western Reserve and generally thought to hold antislavery views. A Democratic faction, of which Salmon P. Chase was the leader, was disgruntled by the failure of the convention to endorse the Wilmot Proviso, but Wood conciliated some of them by taking a strong antislavery position in his only public speech in the campaign. The result of the campaign was Wood's election by a plurality over William Johnston, the Whig candidate, and Edward Smith, a Free Soiler; his vote was 133,093 to 121,105 and 13,747 respectively for his opponents.

The new governor, the first Democrat to be elected to the office since 1842, was a native of Vermont. Born at Middletown in Rutland County in 1792 or 1793, he was the oldest son of the Rev. Nathaniel

Wood, who had served as a chaplain in the continental army during the Revolution. Reuben received his early education at home, but after his father's death he went at the age of fifteen to live with an uncle in Canada, where he pursued studies in the classics and the law. At the outbreak of the War of 1812 he was conscripted into the Canadian army but made his escape in a hazardous crossing of Lake Ontario in a small boat with another American. He served for a short time in the American army and at the close of the war returned home to aid his widowed mother on the farm. He also taught school and completed his legal studies under James Clark of Middletown.

In 1816 Wood married Mary Rice, a daughter of Truman Rice of Clarendon, Vermont, and two years later moved to Cleveland, Ohio. He is said to have arrived in the town with his wife and infant daughter and only a dollar and a quarter in his pocket. So poor was he that, when qualified for admission to the bar, he walked from Cleveland to Ravenna, where the supreme court was in session, to receive his certificate. Cleveland at that time was a village of six hundred and probably had only two other practicing attorneys, Alfred Kelley and Leonard Case.

Through his energy and ability Wood soon gained a wide reputation and was drawn into politics. His first public office was that of state senator, to which he was elected three times, serving continuously from 1825 through 1830. In the latter year he was elected by the general assembly president judge of the court of common pleas for the third judicial circuit, which included Cuyahoga County. In 1832 and again in 1839 Wood was elected a judge of the state supreme court, thus serving two terms (February 1833 to February 1847). There was some objection by the radical antibank Democrats to his reelection in 1839, but they withdrew opposition when they learned that he believed the United States Bank unconstitutional, favored an independent treasury, and held that bank charters were not in the nature of contracts and could be revoked for cause. The Whigs defeated his reelection to a third term in 1847.

When Wood was inaugurated governor in December 1850, the constitutional convention was in progress. The convention completed its work the following March, and the new constitution was adopted at a popular election on June 17 and became effective on the first of September. This document provided for the electing of officials in odd-numbered years, thus limiting the incumbent governor's term to one year. Governor Wood was reelected in the fall of 1851 for a second term with a wide margin over Samuel F. Vinton, the Whig candidate. The Free Soil candidate, Samuel Lewis, polled only 16,914 votes to 119,596 for Vinton, and 145,604 for Wood. The Free Soilers, however, held the balance of power in the general assembly, which was nearly evenly divided between the two major parties.

Governor Wood took a firm stand on the questions of the day. He was strongly opposed to the fugitive slave laws but would not countenance acts of violence in circumventing them. In general he favored the hard-money platform of his party and believed that banks should be taxed at the same rates as individuals, but was not a radical antibank man. Several noteworthy events mark his administration: the burning of the old statehouse, February 1, 1852 (the present building was under construction); the visit to Ohio of Jenny Lind, the Swedish Nightingale; the triumphal tour of the state by Louis Kossuth and his official reception by the Ohio General Assembly on February 7, 1851, on which occasion Kossuth, Governor Wood, and others made addresses.

Of great significance is the mass of new legislation passed by the assembly during his second term to carry into effect the provisions of the constitution of 1851. Among the more important laws were those reorganizing the courts, the need for which was urged by Wood in his first annual message.

In 1853 Governor Wood resigned to become the American consul at Valparaiso, Chile, where he remained until 1855, when he returned to Cleveland to practice law. Soon thereafter he retired to his beautiful farm, "Evergreen Place," near Rockport, Cuyahoga County, and engaged in farming until his death on October 1, 1864. He was a strong Union man and had been scheduled to preside at a Lincoln rally held a few days after his death. He was buried in a lovely spot on his farm, but the body was later removed to Woodlawn Cemetery, Cleveland. His wife and two daughters survived.

As an individual, Reuben Wood was energetic and forceful. He was a capable lawyer, a conscientious legislator, and an excellent trial judge. His tall, lean frame gave him the nickname, "Old Chief of the Cuyahogas." As judge and governor during a critical period in the state's history, he served Ohio well.

The Ohio Historical Society   S. WINIFRED SMITH

WILLIAM MEDILL
1853 - 1856

When Reuben Wood resigned as governor on July 13, 1853, to accept a federal diplomatic appointment, Lieutenant Governor William Medill, according to the rule of succession established by the new state constitution, became Ohio's twenty-second chief executive.

William Medill was born at Whitely Creek Hundred in New Castle County, Delaware, in February of 1802. Of Irish extraction, his parents, William and Isabella Medill, had emigrated to the United States a few years before. Opportunities for the education of farm lads were not very plentiful, but young William completed preparatory studies satisfactorily for entrance in a nearby academy. He taught school and engaged in "other employments" for about six months to pay expenses to attend the Newark Academy (later Delaware College and now the University of Delaware) for the balance of the year. After graduation in 1825, Medill read law on a part-time basis in the office of Judge Black in New Castle, and was admitted to the bar in Delaware in the summer of 1830.

That winter Medill moved to Lancaster, Ohio. An Ohio law required a year's residence in the state, however, before a person could be admitted to practice. He spent most of the year reading in the office of Judge Philemon Beecher of that town and was admitted to the Ohio bar in early 1832.

The people of Fairfield County elected Medill as their representative to the state legislature in 1835, and reelected him for three succeeding terms. His ability as a presiding officer was recognized by his legislative colleagues when he was chosen as the speaker of the house in his third term. In 1838 Fairfield, Perry, Morgan, and Hocking counties elected Medill as their district representative in congress. Reelection in 1840 sent him back for a second term. In this session he committed himself as an antibank Democrat. He was defeated for a third term in 1842.

From President Polk, Medill received an appointment in 1845 as second assistant postmaster general. After a few months he resigned to accept appointment as commissioner of Indian affairs, a position in which he served for the remainder of the Polk administration. The Indians generally held him in high regard for his reforms and justice towards them. It was under his administration that Indian affairs were transferred from the war to the interior department.

Medill was chosen as a delegate to the state constitutional convention held in 1850-51. The strength of the Democratic party in the convention and his position of prominence within the party gained for him on the first ballot the important position as president of that body. As had Edward Tiffin, who presided over the first state constitutional convention a half century before, Medill later became the chief executive of the state. In fact, he was the only member of the 1850-51 convention who rose to that position. The convention produced a constitution which, although a great improvement over the previous one, did not recognize that agrarianism was being replaced by a new economic order.

Under the new constitution the position of lieutenant governor was created. Following the pattern of the federal government, he was also presiding officer of the senate. In the autumn election of 1851, Medill became the first person in Ohio to fill that post. He was chosen by a greater plurality than was Reuben Wood, who was reelected governor. As lieutenant governor, Medill presided over the regular and adjourned sessions of the senate in 1852 and 1853.

On July 13, 1853, Governor Wood resigned to accept a federal appointment as a consular officer in Chile. Upon the resignation of the chief executive, the new constitution provided that "the powers and duties of the office . . . shall devolve upon the lieutenant-governor." William Medill thus became governor.

The Democratic party was victor in the 1853 state elections, and Medill, who had been nominated by a bare majority of three votes, became governor in his own right. The other elective state officials, however, received greater pluralities than he. It is interesting to note that his Whig and abolitionist opponents were the last Whig and abolitionist candidates for governor in Ohio. Medill himself was the last Democratic candidate to be elected for twenty years.

Although there was a substanial majority of Democrats in both houses, no laws of great importance were enacted by the fifty-first general assembly. A resolution was adopted favoring construction of a railroad with Mississippi River and west coast termini. Medill believed that the state should withdraw from its many economic activities and advocated sale of all state-owned canal, turnpike, and railroad stock. No immediate steps were taken, but successive administrations used his position as a basis for action.

The mid-1850's witnessed considerable agitation against foreign and non-Protestant peoples in the United States. These movements found expression in the formation of minority parties which agitated and encouraged clashes and riots, especially in urban centers of foreign and Catholic strength. In city elections in Cincinnati in 1855, riots attained such proportions that the personal presence of the governor and a threat to call out the militia were necessary to quell the disturbance.

The newly formed state Republican party, opposed to the extension of slavery in the federal territories, entered the 1855 contest under the leadership of Salmon P. Chase, who had an antislavery record. Medill ran against him and was defeated by nearly sixteen thousand votes.

The new national Democratic administration appointed Medill as comptroller of the federal treasury. He served in this capacity for almost the entire term of President Buchanan. He performed a notable service by successfully resisting payment of about two million dollars for a claim he felt not justified, in spite of instructions from congress to the contrary and threats of impeachment.

His poor health precluded much activity, and at the end of the Buchanan administration he retired from politics and returned to

Lancaster. In 1863, as a Peace Democrat, he presided over the state convention of his party. In spite of efforts to the contrary he was unable to prevent the gubernatorial nomination of Clement L. Vallandigham, whom he had himself defeated in the nomination for lieutenant governor in 1852. A "slowly consuming and painful but mortal disease" brought death on September 2, 1865. Medill, although "always something of a laides' man and popular in society," had never married. Upon his death his estate passed to his nephew and namesake of Lancaster.

Medill devoted his life to public service and acquitted himself well. He was a man of strict integrity and high character who earned the respect of his political enemies as well as his political associates.

Miami University   DWIGHT L. SMITH

SALMON P. CHASE
1856 - 1860

In 1856 Salmon Portland Chase became the first Republican governor of Ohio as a result of what may truthfully be called a party revolution. The immediate cause of the death of one old party, the Whig, and the birth of two new ones, the Republican and Know-Nothing, was the passage in 1854 of the Kansas-Nebraska Act.

Chase came before the people of Ohio with a long record of implacable opposition to slavery extension. Born in 1808 in Cornish, New Hampshire, of good New England stock, he first came to Ohio as a boy of twelve to live with his uncle, Bishop Philander Chase, who resided in Worthington. After about three years' tutelage under the bishop, first at Worthington and later at Cincinnati, Chase returned to his native state, where he entered Dartmouth College. Following his graduation in 1826 he went to Washington, D. C., where he taught school and read law under the nominal guidance of William Wirt, a distinguished Virginian, who was attorney general in the administration of John Quincy Adams. In 1830 Chase was admitted to the bar and returned to Cincinnati to begin his legal and political career.

Though nominally a Whig, Chase soon became convinced that the slavery issue transcended all others in importance. This conviction led him naturally into the Liberty party and later into the Free Soil party. In 1849, through a coalition of Free Soilers and Democrats in the Ohio assembly, Chase was elected to the United States Senate. There he won national recognition as an opponent of the Compromise of 1850 and the Kansas-Nebraska bill. As a result of his forthright stand on the slavery question he naturally assumed a position of leadership in the rapidly growing anti-Nebraska, or fusionist, movement. Meeting at Columbus on July 13, 1855, the fusionists formally organized the Republican party and chose Chase as their candidate for governor.

The campaign of 1855 was one of exceptional bitterness. Chase's opponents, Governor William Medill, Democrat, and former Governor Allen Trimble, running as the candidate of a die-hard Know-Nothing remnant, charged him with favoring abolitionism, Negro equality, and disunion. Ignoring his detractors, Chase emphasized the dangers of slavery extension and what he called "Southernism." The result of the election, crucial for the future of the Republican party in Ohio, was a victory for the entire Republican ticket.

The Republican administration under Chase represented an artful blending of antislavery radicalism and economic conservatism. The ardent antislavery elements of the new party were appeased by the reelection of Benjamin F. Wade to the senate, the enactment of personal liberty laws, and the passage of strong antislavery resolutions. As for economic measures, under the skillful guidance of a veteran Whig legislator, Alfred Kelley, a law was passed exempting banks from taxation where their charters so provided and permitting deductions of debts from credits for all taxpayers. A new general banking law was passed also but was subject to popular referendum, as provided in the constitution of the state. Although favored by Governor Chase and a number of both Republican and Democratic leaders, the new general banking law was turned down by a majority of voters.

While the assembly was carrying out its program, Chase proceeded with vigor to exercise the limited prerogatives of his office. He skillfully managed the patronage and carried out a much needed reform of the state militia that proved its worth in 1861. He advocated the establishment of a geological survey, a bureau of statistics, and a railroad commission, the improvement of the status of women with regard to property holding, and better opportunities for the common schools and higher education.

Although he had no desire for a second term as governor, Chase was practically forced to run again in 1857 by the misconduct of the treasurer of the state. This official became involved in the misappropriation of about $550,000 of state funds. When the blame for the defalcation was placed on the Republican administration, Chase, stimulated rather than cowed by this challenge to his integrity, stood for reelection and conducted a vigorous campaign throughout the state. By a slim margin the electorate returned him to the governorship but sent a majority of Democrats to the general assembly. The Democrats then proceeded to repeal the personal liberty laws and to enact anti-Negro legislation, attempted to tax banks without regard to their charters, and passed an independent treasury act to divorce the state treasury from banks. The governor remonstrated against most of these measures, but lacking a veto he was powerless to prevent their passage.

When in 1859 the Republicans carried the state offices by substantial majorities and proceeded to return Chase to the United States Senate, his chances for the Republican nomination for president in 1860 seemed promising. But at the Republican convention the Ohio delegation was divided and on the third ballot transferred four votes to Lincoln, which gave him the necessary majority. After the election Chase was appointed secretary of the treasury. While remaining a member of the cabinet Chase allowed himself to become the center of an oust-Lincoln movment. Tension between the president and his finance minister mounted, and when in 1864 the secretary submitted his resignation for the fourth, or perhaps fifth, time, the president accepted it, much to the chagrin of the secretary. Then, when Chief Justice Taney died on October 21, 1864, Lincoln appointed Chase to the highest judicial post in the land.

If, as some historians have suggested, Lincoln's motive in appointing Chase to the court was to put a perennial candidate in an office that would satisfy his ambition and thus "bury" him, as Chase's daughter charged, Lincoln failed, for Chase, abandoning the Republican party, actively sought the Democratic nomination in 1868. In his bid for the presidency he had the aid of his brilliant, beautiful, and wealthy daughter, Kate Chase Sprague, who, as Washington's most lavish hostess, sought to promote his advancement. In spite of the combined efforts of father and daughter, Chase never suceeded in capturing the great prize. Chase's arduous duties as chief justice and fruitless exertions to gain the presidency led to rapid decline in health and to death on May 7, 1873, at the age of sixty-five. He was survived by two daughters, Mrs. Sprague and Mrs. William S. Hoyt.

The Ohio State University   Harry L. Coles, Jr.

WILLIAM DENNISON, JR.
1860 - 1862

William Dennison, Jr., Ohio's twenty-four governor and the first to hold office during the Civil War, was born at Cincinnati November 23, 1815. He was descended from a New England family named Carter through his mother, Mary, while his father, William, was a native of New Jersey. The couple migrated from the latter state to Ohio a decade before their son's birth and settled at Cincinnati where the elder Dennison became a successful business man.

As a student at Miami University, the son displayed outstanding ability in the fields of history, government, and literature. Having been graduated at the age of nineteen, Dennison entered the office of Nathaniel G. Pendleton, the father of George H. Pendleton, and began the study of law. In 1840 he was admitted to the bar, whereupon he became a practicing attorney. After a short time, the young lawyer moved to Columbus and married the eldest daughter of William Neil, a well-known promoter of stage transportation.

Dennison's popularity grew apace with his legal practice, and by 1848 he had become so prominent that the Whigs of Franklin and Delaware counties elected him to the Ohio Senate. His colleagues in the upper house nearly succeeded in elevating him to the speakership but finally failed after a bitter two-week struggle during which the senate was unable even to organize. Dennison appeared on the political scene at a time when the slavery controversy was rapidly approaching a critical stage. The intensity of the struggle demanded partisanship from everyone in public life—there was no neutrality on the issue of slavery—and Dennison put himself indelibly on record four years before his election when he opposed the admission of Texas and the extension of slavery. This action delineated the course he was to follow during the next twenty years.

His record as a legislator was founded firmly on Whig doctrines, with the emphasis on antislavery principles. He was especially vocal in advocating abolition of the slave trade in the District of Columbia and application of the Ordinance of 1787 to all United States territories. Ohio's notorious "Black Laws," however, were the target of his most vigorous onslaughts. These measures imposed upon Negroes discriminatory qualifications for residence and denied them certain rights and privileges. Dennison participated in the campaign to repeal these statutes. Success came in 1849 but only through a political bargain as a result of which the "Black Laws" were repealed and Salmon P. Chase, the prominent opponent of slavery was elected to the United States Senate, while two posts on the state supreme court went to Democrats.

After one term in office Dennison returned to his private practice. For a half dozen years his political activities were subservient to other considerations, although in 1852 he was a presidential elector on the Whig ticket. His attention during this period turned to the spheres of finance and transportation, leading to his selection as president, first of the Exchange Bank of Columbus and then of the Columbus and Xenia Railroad. His interest in railroads continued throughout his life.

Dennison was drawn back into politics in February 1856, when, as one of the first prominent Whigs to become a Republican, he attended the new party's preliminary convention at Pittsburgh and served on the committee on resolutions. In June he acted as chairman of the Ohio delegation to the nominating convention at Philadelphia which chose John C. Frémont as its candidate. Dennison's star continued to ascend,

reaching a new height in 1859 with his nomination by acclamation for
the governorship. Formidable opposition was provided by Supreme Court
Judge Rufus P. Ranney, a man of unquestioned character and integrity.
The candidates conducted a constructive campaign during which they
engaged in a series of public debates throughout the state. Affairs were
further enlivened by the appearance of both Abraham Lincoln and
Stephen A. Douglas, each of whom addressed audiences in three Ohio
cities. The temper of the times was reflected in the outcome, which saw
Dennison victorious by a margin of 13,000 votes.

An administration which began auspiciously enough on January 9,
1860, was destined to become one fraught with greater problems than
those of any previous governor. Dennison had served little more than
half his term when the nation was plunged into civil war. Recognizing
that speed was imperative he assumed emergency powers and acted
unhesitatingly and decisively—his critics said dictatorially. He virtually
commandeered railroads, express companies, and telegraph lines; ignoring
the advice of his attorney-general, he used funds with which the state
had been reimbursed by the federal government for military expenditures
without first turning the money into the treasury; and he dispatched
youthful George McClellan to western Virginia with a body of state
troops to help drive out the Confederates.

His wisdom and foresight were appreciated by few and condemned
by the majority. Despite his victory at the polls, Dennison lacked the
confidence of the people once the war began. A courteous and refined
gentleman, he was an authority on railroad operation and on banking
but totally unequipped to cope with military problems. His faults were
exaggerated and many of the blunders made were committed by
subordinates. Although as chief executive, Dennison accepted responsibility for all shortcomings, perhaps his only serious personal error was his
failure to reorganize his administration immediately. It is doubtful
whether any of his predecessors could have met the issues any more
successfully.

Dennison's renomination, a virtual certainty before the outbreak
of hostilities, became a political impossibility. The party leaders, seeking
the cooperation of the War Democrats, chose David Tod as their
standard-bearer in the 1861 election. Dennison accepted this turn of
events with stoic equanimity. His loyalty to the party did not waver, and
Governor Tod constantly called upon him for advice and assistance.

Recognition of his contributions came in 1864 when he was named chairman of the Republican national convention. A few months later President Lincoln appointed him postmaster general, a post which he held until he found himself in serious disagreement with President Johnson's policies in 1866. Although he occupied no other elective or major appointive position, Dennison long remained a figure to be reckoned with in state and national politics. He was a potential vice-presidential nominee in 1872, and eight years later he unsuccessfully opposed Garfield for the Republican senatorial nomination. Also in 1880, the former governor captained the Sherman forces in Ohio and at the national convention.

Business and civic interests claimed much of Dennison's time in his declining years. In addition to his fiscal and transportation operations, he made his influence felt in other fields through his position as city councilman, organizer of the Franklin County Agricultural Society, and promoter of such industries as the Columbus Rolling Mills. Dennison acquired considerable wealth from his several investments and, despite losses as a result of the Panic of 1873, he lived out his remaining years in easy circumstances.

When death came on June 15, 1882, after an eighteen-month illness, Dennison was regarded as Columbus' leading citizen. His wife and seven children survived him. His life had been a constructive and useful one. While he excelled in the economic field, he was perhaps only adequate as a statesman but his honesty was never questioned. To a great extent the victim of circumstances as governor, Dennison has been treated with more sympathy by later generations than by his contemporaries.

The Ohio Historical Society   JOHN S. STILL

DAVID TOD
1862 - 1864

True to its intention of holding a Union party convention in the summer of 1861, the Republican party of Ohio did not issue instructions for the election of delegates. Instead, the call came from a public appeal signed by one hundred prominent Ohioans who represented several shades of political philosophy. However, the men had at least one thing in common: they all supported the war. David Tod, previously a radical Democrat, not only affixed his name to the call but emerged from the convention as the Union party's nominee for governor.

To the delegates at the convention, as to most Ohioans, Tod was well known. Son of Judge George Tod, he was born in Youngstown on February 21, 1805. David Tod began practicing law in 1827 and five years later was appointed postmaster of Warren. In 1832 he married Maria Smith who became the mother of his seven children.

An ardent Democrat in a stronghold of Western Reserve Whiggery, Tod ran for the Ohio Senate in 1838 and gained election. During his term as a senator he helped secure approval of antibanking legislation and figured prominently in the passage of a bill to facilitate the return

80

of fugitive slaves to their masters in Kentucky. He also was instrumental in defeating Thomas Morris, antislavery Democrat, for reelection as United States Senator and electing Benjamin Tappan in his place.

Tod did not run for another term; instead, he returned to his law practice. But his party work in the campaigns of 1840 and 1842 earned him the title of "giant of Democracy," and qualified him as an expert Whig "coonskinner." Despite these laurels, he failed to gain victory as the Democratic candidate for governor in two consecutive campaigns. Running on violent antibank platforms, Tod lost to Mordecai Bartley in 1844 and William Bebb in 1846. Both defeated him by a slender margin.

In March 1847 President Polk appointed Tod as minister to Brazil, a post in which he served with distinction until 1851. Returning to Youngstown, Tod gave full attention to his growing coal, iron, and railroad interests—interests in which he accumulated a fortune. Throughout the 1850's Tod regarded himself more of a party patriarch than active campaigner; however, through an odd circumstance his district nominated him for congress in 1858. Pressing business affairs allowed him to show but little interest in the campaign and he lost decisively to his Republican opponent, John Hutchins.

Under the gathering war clouds of sectionalism in 1860, Tod served as a delegate to the Democratic national convention at Charleston. After the convention moved to Baltimore and became deadlocked, he succeeded Caleb Cushing as chairman. Tod was instrumental in securing the nomination of Stephen A. Douglas, and later strenuously stumped for his election.

Following Lincoln's election and the outbreak of civil strife, the lifelong Democrat turned his back to his party, made public appeals for political unity, and wholeheartedly supported Lincoln and the war. Thus he was the logical Union party choice for governor. In a listless campaign, in which the war took precedence over politics, Tod overwhelmingly defeated Democrat Hugh J. Jewett by a margin of over 50,000 votes.

During the first few months of his administration Governor Tod faced few duties other than continuing the work of his predecessor, William Dennison. But soon, as the war pressed more directly upon the state, he became occupied with an array of problems. Ohio's troops suffered heavily in the battle of Shiloh in April 1862, and the governor quickly dispatched aid to the wounded. This service he continued throughout his term. Also, Tod established various agencies in the North to meet soldiers' difficulties relative to transporation, pay, sickness, and disability. Recruiting became more trying as patriotism faltered, and Tod's appeals for volunteers changed to orders for drafting. Confederate troops threatened Ohio twice during 1862. But Tod's speedy action for border defense—aided by the famous "Squirrel Hunters"—sealed the state against invasion.

Politically, however, his first year was not successful. General dissatisfaction with the war's progress, political arrests, and the preliminary Emancipation Proclamation contributed to the Union party's defeat in the state elections of 1862. The Democrats captured all state offices at stake and fourteen of the nineteen seats to the national congress. Encouraged by these results, Ohio's Copperheads fanned the flames of the "fire in the rear." Tod had to contend with outbreaks of armed resistance in Holmes and Noble counties, and faced kidnapping and civil suits brought against him by Edson B. Olds, whom Tod had had arrested and imprisoned. Military authorities quelled the civil disturbances; the legal questions never reached trial. More serious than any of these, however, was the Morgan raid into Ohio. The governor's hurried assemblage of a large number of troops discouraged Confederate attacks on Columbus or any of the prison camps. Although the raid proved to be of little military consequence, Morgan's men did considerable plundering. Tod instructed the county military committees to assess the damage and subsequently the legislature voted funds to individual sufferers.

Tod ardently desired a second term and made an active canvass for it. Union party managers, however, disliked the frequency with which he filled vacancies with old Democratic friends. Furthermore, Tod was rather cool towards emancipation. These considerations robbed him of Union League support and resulted in the nomination of John Brough.

Tod held no other official position, although in June 1864 Lincoln offered him the post of secretary of the treasury. Because of ill health, he declined. He had been troubled for years with strokes of apoplexy, and it was from such an attack that he died in November 1868.

His administration was characterized by intense patriotism, devotion to duty, administrative ability, and unflagging energy. Ohio was fortunate to have had David Tod as one of its war governors.

Wright Air Development Center, Dayton   DELMER J. TRESTER

JOHN BROUGH
1864 - 1865

Born on September 17, 1811, at Marietta, the son of an English immigrant and a Pennsylvania mother, John Brough rose on the tide of Jacksonian democracy. Left an orphan at eleven, he apprenticed himself to a printer for his board and room and in the office of the *American Friend* first smelled the printer's ink which was to bear him into the political arena. The Marietta schools and three years as a part-time student at Ohio University were the extent of his formal schooling. While attending the latter institution, he worked as a reporter on the *Athens Mirror*.

The *Western Republican* of Marietta, which he owned from 1831 to 1833, was his first newspaper. Strongly Jacksonian in its editorial accents, it helped to crystallize his political views. In 1833 he and his brother Charles purchased the *Ohio Eagle* at Lancaster which carried on the Democratic tradition.

In 1835 Brough gained election as clerk of the Ohio Senate by a margin of one vote. While holding this position he was capitol correspondent for his own paper and for the *Ohio Statesman.* In 1837 the Whigs deposed him, though he continued to have the strong support of Samuel Medary and the Democratic party. His stand in 1837 paralleled that of the national administration. He denounced the Whig attitude toward banks as a betrayal of the people and a surrender to moneyed interests. As a result he was elected to the general assembly from the Fairfield-Hocking district in 1838 and immediately became chairman of the committee on banks and currency in the house.

Governor Shannon's inaugural address sounded the alarm on the over-issue of bank notes and speculation. Brough's committee immediately offered resolutions in the house which would stabilize the finances of the state. It also requested the auditor to report on conditions in state banks, and asked for power to investigate irregularities in banking practices. Brough himself introduced a bill which would have prohibited the establishment of any national bank, corporation, or agency of the federal government in Ohio which was not incorporated under its laws. He also offered what he felt were constructive solutions to the currency problems. He proposed a broader application of individual liability on the part of directors and stockholders of banks, but his bill failed passage as did his recommendations to outlaw the national bank, usury, and currency speculation. He successfully defeated the Whig scheme to establish state banks with state capital, and expressed the view that banking growth should be in relation to the expansion of trade and commerce.

His firm stand on financial affairs won him the state auditorship in 1839. As auditor he tried to carry out a policy of strong banks, financial honesty and integrity, and hard currency. The effects of the Panic of 1837 were still evident. There was a steadily increasing state debt, which mounted from $12,500,000 to nearly $20,000,000 during his auditorship. In spite of this, Brough fought to stay speculation and inflation, to punish dishonesty, to defeat the sentiment for repudiation, and to secure payment of the indebtedness. In all of these he succeeded. The canals were completed and began to produce revenue, banks were saved from failure by close examination, and taxes were increased five mills per dollar with safety. However, the sweeping victory of the Whigs in 1844 numbered the days of John Brough as auditor.

From the end of his last term as auditor until his election to the governorship, Brough played no direct role in politics. In 1841 he and his brother had bought the Cincinnati *Advertiser* and renamed it the *Enquirer.* After his political retirement he was its editor until he became president of the Madison and Indianapolis Railway in 1848.

At the outbreak of the Civil War, Brough broke from strictly Democratic politics, though he continued his opposition to the Republican party. A speech at Marietta on June 10, 1863, again brought him into the political limelight. Backed by William Henry Smith of the *Cincinnati Gazette,* Brough became the standard-bearer against growing copper-headism, and was elected governor in the fall of that year over Clement L. Vallandigham.

As governor, he pledged his support to the Union and the successful prosecution of the war. He secured the passage of a levy of two mills on the dollar for public support of servicemen's families, and of the right of an additional one and one-half mills to be levied by city and county administrations as they saw fit. He helped to furnish troops for the army, sent the national guard into federal service for the "good of the nation," brought into effect a fair system of officer promotion among Ohio troops, and provided for inspection of field hospitals and better medical care.

When Salmon P. Chase resigned as secretary of the treasury, Brough was offered the position but declined it. In the election of 1864 he opposed McClellan and the "Peace Democrats" and threw his support to Lincoln, not as a Republican, but as a symbol of union.

In the spring of 1865 Brough announced that because of failing health he would not seek renomination. In August, four months before the expiration of his term of office, he died in Cleveland. Governor Brough was twice married and had seven children.

Whatever may be said of Brough's partisanship and his lack of personal dignity, one must assess in his favor the qualities of integrity, perseverance, and public spiritedness. At two of the most trying periods of nineteenth century Ohio history, John Brough worked avidly to bring problems to solution. As newspaperman, state auditor, railway executive, and governor, Brough performed his duties with ability and tireless effort.

Anthony Wayne Parkway Board RICHARD C. KNOPF

CHARLES ANDERSON
1865 - 1866

The twenty-seventh governor of Ohio, Charles Anderson, filled the vacancy created by John Brough's death. Although he spent less than five months as governor, Anderson served his adopted state well in other capacities.

At his father's residence, "Soldier's Retreat," near the falls of the Ohio River and within the present-day city limits of Louisville, Kentucky, Charles Anderson was born on June 1, 1814. His father, Colonel Richard Clough Anderson, who had served as aide-de-camp to Lafayette in the American Revolution, migrated from Virginia in 1783 to become a land surveyor in the Virginia Military District of Ohio. His headquarters was at Louisville. Anderson's mother was related to Chief Justice John Marshall.

In 1829 Anderson entered Miami University where it is said he "prosecuted his studies, both in the English branches and in the ancient classics." He was "educated in a liberal manner" and graduated in 1833.

It had been his boyhood ambition to become a farmer in the vicinity of St. Louis, but he gave this up to read law in the office of Pirtle and Anderson in Louisville.

He was admitted to the bar in 1835 and moved to Dayton, Ohio, where he decided to open a law office. That autumn he was married to Eliza J. Brown, the daughter of a Dayton merchant who had served with Anthony Wayne in the West. Anderson's law practice in Dayton was supplemented by a farm and by service for a term as prosecuting attorney of Montgomery County.

In 1844 Anderson was elected to the Ohio Senate. Here he established himself as a champion of Negro rights. A pioneer advocate of the repeal of Ohio's "Black Laws," he worked tirelessly for that end but not very successfully. He was also one of the leaders in the efforts to complete the new statehouse. At the expiration of his term, Anderson spent several months touring Europe and taking the "water cure" at an Austrian resort.

Back in Ohio, Anderson moved with his family to Cincinnati in 1848. Here he entered into a law partnership with Rufus King which soon grew into a "large and successful" business. Once more, however, in 1855 or 1856, Anderson moved back to Dayton. Poor health convinced him that he should seek a different climate, and in 1859 he moved to Texas and managed farm property which he had purchased there.

In Texas he found the people greatly excited over the political situation in the country and seriously entertaining the possibility of secession. In the midst of the election year of 1860, Anderson addressed a large gathering in San Antonio, boldly calling for the "perpetuity of the national Union." For this he gained many enemies and received a number of threatening letters. After the Civil War broke out, Anderson disposed of his property and set out with his family to leave the country by way of Mexico. En route he was arrested without any charge and taken back to San Antonio as a political prisoner. Not long after, he escaped, overtook his family in Mexico, and returned to Dayton.

President Lincoln sent Anderson on a special mission to England to lecture in behalf of the cause of the Union. Discouraged, he soon returned to the United States to serve in a more effective way. His services were accepted by the governor of Ohio, who appointed him a colonel and commander of the 93d Ohio Volunteer Infantry, which was being organized in the summer of 1862. At the battle of Stone

River, serving under General Rosecrans, Anderson was severely wounded. Not expecting to live, he resigned his commission and returned home.

He recovered, however, and ran successfully for lieutenant governor in 1863 on the Union ticket with John Brough. In this capacity he served in the regular and adjourned sessions of the fifty-sixth general assembly in 1864 and 1865 which devoted their attention primarily to measures concerning the war.

Governor Brough died on August 29, 1865, and Anderson acceded to his office. The few months in which he served as governor, August 29, 1865, to January 8, 1866, were uneventful, and "the services he performed were merely routine." Afterwards he returned to his law practice in Dayton.

The lure of rural life which had always attracted him once more prevailed, and in 1870 he settled on a large estate on the Cumberland River in Lyon County, Kentucky. There he died at Kuttawa, a village which he had founded, on September 2, 1895. He was survived by a son and two daughters.

Governor Anderson and his brothers had served their country well. His eldest brother, Richard, served a term in congress, was the first United States minister to Columbia, and was a commissioner to the Panama Congress. Another brother, Robert, a West Point graduate, was in command at Fort Sumter at the outbreak of the Civil War.

Anderson was well known as a lawyer and as a plain-spoken orator. He was described as "tall and elegant in person" and as an "accomplished Christian gentleman."

Miami University   DWIGHT L. SMITH

JACOB D. COX
1866 - 1868

Jacob Dolson Cox, twenty-eighth governor of Ohio, was born October 27, 1828, in Montreal, Canada, where his father, a well-known New York contractor, was superintending the roof construction of the Church of Notre Dame. The father, American-born, was of German descent; his wife, Thedia Redelia Kenyon, was a New Englander who counted Elder William Brewster among her ancestors. At home they encouraged a feeling for art and music, a strong religious sentiment, and an almost Puritanical sense of conscience and integrity. Young Jacob's education was less well-ordered than his home life: he spent a few terms at a private school and a year with a classically educated minister, and then did private reading with a Columbia College student. At fourteen he began his practical education as an articled clerk in a law office, and at sixteen entered a brokerage firm to learn bookkeeping and business procedures.

About this time Jacob thought of going to sea. His plans were changed, however, by the arrival of the Rev. Samuel D. Cochran, an

Oberlin College graduate, who came to New York to establish a Congregational church. Jacob's mother and oldest sisters joined the church, and soon after, during a series of the Rev. Charles G. Finney's revival meetings at Niblo's Theater, Jacob joined too and decided to study for the ministry. Through the influence of Cochran and Finney, young Cox then began his long relationship with Oberlin College, terminated by his service as a trustee, 1876-1900. After a year in the academy and three years in the college he was graduated in 1850. Part of his expenses he earned by baking bread at the college boarding house, and during one year he received 18¾ cents an hour for teaching algebra. Literary societies and musical organizations claimed his extracurricular time, although he apparently socialized, too, for an Oberlin co-ed wrote a friend to report: "There is some good folks here, and some slick *fellers* too, one in particular, a Mr. Cox from New York City."

During his college career, Cox fell in love with President Finney's eldest daughter, at nineteen a widow with a small son. On Thanksgiving Day, 1849, they were married, and Cox moved into his father-in-law's house, while Finney made a preaching tour of England. Upon Finney's return he was distressed to find Cox, now a graduate student of theology, viewing the strict Oberlin doctrines somewhat more critically than was customary, and the two exchanged words that made it awkward for Cox to remain in Oberlin.

Thereupon he took a position as superintendent of schools in Warren, resumed his study of law, and in 1853 was admitted to the bar. Soon he developed an extensive practice and became a popular citizen of the community, leading the Choral Union, as well as the Presbyterian church choir, and organizing a literary society. By 1855 he was helping organize the Republican party in Warren and stumping through Trumbull and nearby counties; four years later he reluctantly accepted a nomination for the Ohio Senate and was elected.

In Columbus, Cox joined James Monroe, an old Oberlin friend, and James A. Garfield to form the "Radical Triumvirate," a potent trio, which, together with Cox's good friend Governor William Dennison, helped shape legislation on the eve of the Civil War. In the spring of 1860 Cox was appointed brigadier general of the Ohio militia, and with Garfield made an intensive study of military science during the 1860-61 session of the legislature.

When the war broke out in 1861, for Cox there was hardly a

moment of indecision; though he was in poor health, heavily in debt, and the father of six children (he was to have two more), he determined to take an active part in the conflict, and accepted an appointment as brigadier general of the Ohio Volunteers. He was first made commander of Camp Jackson, a recruit depot near Columbus, where among his charges were many college boys, including one company under the colonelcy of President Lorin Andrews of Kenyon and the "praying company" from Oberlin.

Within a few months Cox began his field service and a record as one of the most brilliant volunteer officers, serving in the Kanawha Valley campaign and at South Mountain, commanding the 9th Army Corps at Antietam and the 23d Army Corps late in the Atlanta, Franklin, and Nashville campaigns, and being commissioned major general in 1864. In later years General Cox became widely known as a military historian, writing several volumes, including two in the *Campaigns of the Civil War* series, and serving as military book critic for *The Nation*. His two-volume *Military Reminiscences of the Civil War* was completed just a few weeks before his death in 1900.

In 1865 the coalition Union party elected its last candidates in Ohio. With a core of 143 soldier delegates, the convention met in Columbus and named three military men among the nine on the state slate, with General Jacob D. Cox at its head. The platform was generally conservative, and endorsed President Johnson's policies toward the seceded states. Although the party ignored the Negro suffrage question, considered vital on the Western Reserve, Cox spoke boldly on the issue, astounding his prewar radical friends by opposing Negro voting and proposing to separate the two races in the South by establishing a large Negro reserve in contiguous territory in South Carolina, Georgia, Alabama, and Florida. Despite Western Reserve opposition, these views apparently reflected the attitudes of returned soldiers, and Cox was easily elected over the still Copperhead-tainted Democratic candidate, General George W. Morgan of Licking County.

Cox's administration was not notable, for the radicals and conservatives within the Republican ranks, with Cox favoring the latter, were badly divided on critical postwar issues, and the result was inaction. Aside from his sponsorship of a centralized board of charities, Cox's chief administrative efforts were to bridge the gap between Ohio radicals and President Johnson. By the time of the 1867 state convention the radicals were in control, and Cox refused to try for renomination.

After his term as governor, Cox moved to Cincinnati to practice law until March 1869, when President Grant appointed him secretary of the interior. Cox resigned after eighteen months, protesting the political assessments levied upon federal employees and general "spoils" practices. The next year there was a brief flurry of interest in the Ohio senatorship, but the legislature reelected the less conservative John Sherman. In 1872 Cox joined the Liberal Republican movement and supported the nomination of Greeley; in 1876, running as a reform Republican, he was elected to congress from the Toledo district, served one term, and then retired from politics. From 1873 to 1878, meanwhile, he had served as president and as receiver of the Toledo and Wabash Railroad Company.

Always a man of scholarly interests, it was while he lived in Toledo that Cox developed an interest in microscopy, studied photomicrography, and began contributing papers to professional journals. In 1881 he was elected a fellow of the Royal Microscopical Society, and in 1884 and again in 1892 was named president. At the Antwerp Exposition in 1891 his achievements were rewarded with the gold medal for excellence in microphotography.

After his congressional term, Cox returned to Cincinnati and in 1881 became dean of the Cincinnati Law School, a post he held until 1897, meanwhile serving from 1885 to 1889 also as president of the University of Cincinnati. Upon Cox's retirement from the deanship, President McKinley urged him to accept the critical post of minister to Spain, but he refused and moved to Oberlin to write his memoirs. He died on August 4, 1900, at Magnolia, Massachusetts. Personally attractive and a man of great integrity, a skilled speaker and writer, an effective administrator, a noted scholar, and an able field general, Jacob Dolson Cox enjoyed one of the most versatile and successful careers of his time.

University of Virginia   J. JEFFERY AUER

RUTHERFORD B. HAYES
1868 - 1872, 1876 - 1877

The spirited gubernatorial campaign in 1867 was launched with a lengthy keynote address, "Union and Liberty," delivered at Lebanon on August 5 by the Union Republican candidate, Rutherford Birchard Hayes of Cincinnati, lawyer and soldier, then serving his second term in congress. The Democratic candidate was Allen G. Thurman of Chillicothe and Columbus, former congressman and chief justice of the Ohio Supreme Court, who was to become a United States Senator and a member of the electoral commission which in 1877 would seat Hayes as president of the United States.

"The campaign was fought over the question of Negro suffrage" and was carried to all parts of the state by both candidates. It attracted national attention. Between August and the election in October, Hayes delivered eighty-one speeches to his opponent's seventy-one, it was said. Hayes won the election by a majority of only 2,983 votes. His "personal popularity, and his wonderful resources," when called upon, "carried him far ahead of the vote of his party," and the legislature chosen was Democratic.

The first term of two years for Governor Hayes met with general approval, and in 1869 his party renominated him by acclamation to run against George H. Pendleton of Cincinnnati, lawyer, state senator, congressman, and subsequently United States Senator and minister to Germany. The election gave Governor Hayes a majority of 7,500 votes over Pendleton.

After his second term as governor ended in 1872, Hayes preferred to remain out of politics. But his party nominated him for congress from the second district of Cincinnati. His opponent was General H. B. Banning of Mount Vernon and Cincinnati. The election went heavily against the Republicans in Hamilton County, and, though Hayes led his ticket by a thousand votes, he was defeated.

On June 2, 1875, much against his personal wishes, the Republicans selected Hayes for the third time as their candidate for governor. His opponent was William Allen of Chillicothe, a former congressman who was then governor of Ohio. Allen had been nominated by the Democrats for "re-election by acclamation, and the tendencies of the times were favorable to his continuance in office, but, after a contest which aroused an interest not only throughout the United States, but in Europe," Hayes became Ohio's first governor to be elected to a third term.

The activities of Hayes as governor of Ohio during his three terms included establishing the Soldiers' and Sailors' Orphans' Home at Xenia; enlarging the powers of the state board of charities; founding the Agricultural and Mechanical College which in 1878 became the Ohio State University; securing minority representation on election boards; and carrying out a program of systematic reduction of the state debt. Also during his governorship the state ratified the fifteenth amendment to the United States Constitution, insuring the vote to all men regardless of race or color.

An active state geological survey program was pushed by Governor Hayes which resulted in numerous reports and geological maps. Hayes believed that "the future growth of Ohio, in wealth and population," would depend largely "on the development of the mining and manufacturing resources of the state." Other of his accomplishments were to add several hundred letters and other manuscripts of various sorts connected with the early history of the state to the collections in the Ohio State Library; to obtain paintings of the portraits of all the governors of the state and of several other distinguished citizens; to purchase a full set of casts of the pottery of the moundbuilder Indians; and to erect a Lincoln and soldiers' memorial in the rotunda of the statehouse.

Governor Hayes also directed public attention to the evils of excessive legislation; to the chaos resulting from the practically unlimited powers then possessed by local authorities to make expenditures and to levy taxes; and to the importance of prohibiting all public debts except those required in time of war or to suppress insurrection or rebellion.

Rutherford B. Hayes was born in Delaware, Ohio, on October 4, 1822, and was educated in the district schools at Delaware; at Norwalk Seminary, Norwalk, Ohio; at Isaac Webb's Maple Grove Academy, Middletown, Connecticut; at Kenyon College; and at the Harvard Law School. He began the practice of law in Lower Sandusky, now Fremont, Ohio, in 1845, where he formed a partnership with Ralph P. Buckland. In 1849 he removed to Cincinnati, then the largest city in the West, to practice law alone for a time. In 1854 he entered into a partnership with William K. Rogers and Richard M. Corwine, which was dissolved in 1858 when he became city solicitor. He was married on December 30, 1852, to Lucy Webb of Chillicothe, a graduate of the Wesleyan Women's College, Cincinnati, by whom he had six children.

At the outbreak of the Civil War, Hayes volunteered as a major in the 23d Regiment, Ohio Volunteer Infantry, serving four years as lieutenant colonel, colonel, and brigadier general, in West Virginia, Virginia, and Maryland. He was wounded four times, once severely in the left arm, at the Battle of South Mountain.

Resigning from the army on June 9, 1865, with the rank of brevet major general of volunteers, Hayes went to Washington as a Republican congressman from the second district of Ohio, a post to which he had been elected while still in the field. When party managers had asked him in 1864 to campaign, he had answered: *"An officer fit for duty who at this crisis would abandon his post to electioneer for a seat in Congress ought to be scalped."*

The years between 1872 and 1875 were the only years Governor Hayes was not in public service since he had entered politics in 1858. These years he devoted to improving his Spiegel Grove estate in Fremont, which had been bequeathed to him by his uncle, Sardis Birchard; to the founding of Birchard Public Library in Fremont; and to the development of his properties in Ohio, Minnesota, and elsewhere.

Governor Hayes served but one year of his third term. He was nominated for president by the Republican party on the seventh ballot at the convention held in Cincinnati in June 1876. The Democratic candidate was Samuel J. Tilden, governor of New York. The Republican and Democratic parties waged a vigorous campaign, in which neither candidate took an active part, and the election was close and contested. It was necessary for congress to establish an electoral commission in order to determine the result, and on March 2, 1877, the commission reached a decision in favor of Hayes.

As president the former Ohio governor was guided by the slogan which he had adopted: *"He serves his party best who serves his country best."* He sought the unification and pacification of the nation, which had been divided for years by the Civil War, by withdrawing troops from occupation duty in the South; he advocated a sound currency; he reformed the civil service by placing merit before political expediency; he developed an Indian policy founded on peace and justice; and in foreign relations he followed a firm but peaceful course, advocating arbitration of disputes between nations.

When President Hayes left the White House after serving only the one term he had agreed upon, he returned to his Spiegel Grove home in Fremont. As a private citizen he became actively engaged in promoting the causes of general and Negro education, prison reform, veterans' affairs, and many other worthy causes for the public good.

Mrs. Hayes died suddenly on June 25, 1889, from a stroke; and he died after an illness of only three days, on the morning of January 17, 1893. Both are buried on a quiet, wooded knoll in Spiegel Grove, now a state memorial.

The Hayes Memorial Library   WATT P. MARCHMAN

EDWARD F. NOYES
1872 - 1874

Edward F. Noyes was born at Haverhill, Massachusetts, on October 3, 1832. Left an orphan at the age of three, he spent his early life in New Hampshire, where he lived with his grandfather and a guardian. At the age of thirteen he was apprenticed to the printer of the *Morning Star,* a religious newspaper published in Dover, New Hampshire. He remained a printer-boy for four and one-half years until he left to enter an academy at Kingston, New Hampshire. In 1853 he enrolled in Dartmouth College.

While in his senior year, Noyes' forensic ability and whole-hearted advocacy of the principles of the newly-founded Republican party were recognized by the Republican state committee of New Hampshire, which selected the youth to speak in support of the election of John C. Frémont to the presidency. This event whetted Noyes' appetite for a future career in politics.

After his graduation from Dartmouth in 1857, fourth in a class of fifty-seven, Noyes visited a classmate in Cincinnati. So taken was the ambitious easterner with the vigorous energy and material progress of the bustling "Queen City," that he remained there to study law with M. E. Curwen, graduating from the Cincinnati Law School in 1858.

With the firing upon Fort Sumter, Noyes turned from his law practice to help raise the 39th Ohio Infantry Regiment. On July 27, 1861, he was commissioned a major in this regiment. For three years he participated in every battle and skirmish in which his command was engaged. One superior officer spoke of Noyes as being "as efficient and faithful as he is brave and determined." Noyes advanced to the rank of colonel as he received commendations from Generals John Pope, William S. Rosecrans, and William T. Sherman, among others.

On July 4, 1864, while in command of an assault near Ruff's Mills, Georgia, Colonel Noyes received an ankle wound which resulted in the amputation of his left leg. Three months later, although Noyes had only partially recovered from his amputation and was yet on crutches, he was assigned by Major General Joseph Hooker to command Camp Dennison, Ohio, and breveted a brigadier general. Here Noyes remained until April 22, 1865, when he resigned to become city solicitor of Cincinnati. Before his term as solicitor expired he was elected in October 1866 to be probate judge of Hamilton County.

In 1871 the Republican party, seeking to retain the votes of thousands of Civil War veterans, chose General Noyes as its candidate for governor. In an unexciting campaign the thirty-nine year old Cincinnatian defeated his Democratic rival, Colonel George W. McCook, by more than twenty thousand votes.

Few measures of general importance were enacted during Noyes' administration. Election laws were amended to make it unlawful for election judges to leave the place of voting or to remove the ballot boxes until after the votes had been tallied. Acts were passed to define more clearly the powers and duties of county officers. Governor Noyes sponsored new inspection laws for coal mines, investigated Ohio's pardon system, made recommendations for fish conservation measures, and secured the division of the Buckeye state into twenty congressional districts.

The year 1873 was a troubled one for Ohio Republicans, still shaken by the abortive Liberal revolt of the preceding year. When a widespread depression settled upon the country, local Republican leaders were bound to pay the political penalty for economic suffering and unemployment. Added to this were the maladministration of the Grant regime, the odium of Crédit Mobilier, and the infamy of the Salary Grab Act, all unjustly attaching themselves to Noyes' campaign for reelection. The gubernatorial contest of 1873 was fierce, as Noyes' aggressive Democratic opponent, the aged William Allen, called by one newspaper, "that marvelous relic of a bygone era of statesmanship," attacked the Republicans for passing laws for the "benefit of corporations, cliques and rings," while the country suffered from their corruption and negligence. The majority was small, but the final vote disclosed that by a scant plurality of 817 votes Ohio had elected a Democratic governor for the first time since the Civil War. Noyes' subsequent bid for the senatorship in 1874 was rejected by the Democratic legislature which elected Allen G. Thurman.

At the Republican national convention of 1876 Governor Noyes was designated by the twenty-five-man Ohio delegation to present the name of Rutherford B. Hayes for the presidency. Noyes' zealous, behind-the-scenes management of Hayes' campaign, described by one veteran observer as "able, judicious, untiring, unselfish, inspiring, adroit," won the support of hesitant independents and reformers and secured Hayes' nomination. Following the uncertain results of the fall elections, Noyes hurriedly joined the "visiting statesmen" sent to observe events in Florida and to advocate the Republican side before the local canvassing board. Amid charges of fraud and incidents of violence, Noyes helped attain his party's victory in Florida. Two years later, a congressional investigating committee absolved Noyes of charges that he had improperly influenced the Florida canvassers by promises of political favor.

In 1877 President Hayes selected Edward Noyes to succeed Elihu B. Washburne as minister to France, a position which Noyes filled for four years with distinction to himself and credit to his country. As minister he represented this country in the Paris Exposition of 1878, participated in the International Monetary Conference held in Paris in the same year for the purpose of fixing international exchange values of gold and silver, and toured Africa in quest of opportunities for American commercial interests. Replaced in 1881 by the New York banker, Levi Parsons Morton, Noyes returned to Cincinnati where he resumed his law practice and served as an elder counselor in the Republican gubernatorial campaigns of the eighties. He died suddenly on September 4, 1890, while serving on the bench of the superior court of Cincinnati, a post to which he had been elected only a year earlier. He was survived by his wife, Margaret, and their son.

Noyes had brought to the governorship and his subsequent positions not only varied and extensive learning in the law, but also a matchless eloquence. He was of commanding and handsome presence, was gifted with a fine voice, and was a master of the graces of rhetoric and the rules of logic. William Henry Smith, writing to Rutherford B. Hayes, referred to Noyes' political conduct as "that of a noble, chivalrous, honorable gentleman."

HAROLD M. HELFMAN
Air Research and Development Command, Baltimore, Maryland

WILLIAM ALLEN
1874 - 1876

William Allen's long political career spanned the ante-bellum and the post-Civil War periods. His Quaker ancestors were among the earliest settlers of Pennsylvania. Allen's branch of the family removed to North Carolina, separated from the Society of Friends, and took an active part in the Revolutionary War. His father, Nathaniel Allen, was an officer in the Revolutionary Army and later was a member of the North Carolina convention which ratified the federal constitution. His mother, Sarah (Colburn) Allen, was the third wife of Colonel Allen. Both parents died shortly after William's birth in 1803, and, through a technicality of the law, he was deprived of his share of the large estate of his father.

Allen was reared by his half-sister, a woman of strong character, who married the Rev. Pleasant Thurman. After a short residence in Lynchburg, Virginia, where Allen was apprenticed to a saddler, the young boy of sixteen determined to seek his fortunes in the West, whither his sister and her family had already gone. In the middle of the winter of 1819 Allen made the perilous journey on foot across the Alleghanies to his sister's home in Chillicothe, Ohio.

After two years of preparation at Chillicothe Academy, supplemented by a course of general reading under the supervision of his sister, Allen began the study of law in Chillicothe in the office of Edward King, the son of Rufus King of New York. Three years later, at the age of twenty-one, Allen was admitted to the bar and began to practice as a partner of King. Allen, according to frontier custom, rode the circuit. His audacity, skill as a debater, and fluency of speech soon won for him a local reputation.

In 1832 Allen was nominated for representative to congress by the Jacksonian Democrats in a district normally Republican. After an exciting campaign, Allen won by a majority of one against General Duncan McArthur, whose daughter, Mrs. Effie Coons, Allen subsequently married in 1842.

Allen served one term in the house but was defeated for reelection. In 1837, however, at the age of thirty-four, Allen was elected by a Democratic state legislature to the United States Senate to succeed Thomas Ewing. In 1843 Allen was reelected for a second term. In the senate he acquired a national reputation as one of the leaders of the Northwest Democrats. He was a severe critic of John Bull and an ardent expansionist. He urged the annexation of Texas and was one of the vociferous advocates of "Fifty-four Forty or Fight" in the Oregon controversy with Great Britain. As chairman of the committee on foreign relations he was President Polk's spokesman during the war with Mexico.

Allen failed, however, to realize the importance and significance of the development of the Free-Soil element in the Democratic party. In 1848 he was suggested as a compromise presidential candidate when the followers of Cass and Van Buren clashed in the Democratic national convention at Baltimore. He refused to become a candidate and supported Cass. After the election he retired to private life. During the Civil War, Allen was a Peace Democrat and a bitter critic of the Lincoln administration.

In 1873 Allen made a spectacular reappearance in state politics. The maladministration of the Grant regime, together with the "hard times" caused by the Panic of 1873, gave the Democrats of Ohio a wonderful opportunity to win the gubernatorial election of that year, provided they could find a suitable candidate. They needed an old-time Democrat who stood high in the party and who was an orator and a man whose honesty was beyond reproach. At the suggestion of his nephew, Senator Allen G. Thurman, the Democrats nominated "Rise Up William Allen," a name given the candidate by a bit of doggerel verse attributed to Murat Halstead and published in the *Cincinnati Commercial*:

> Come rise up William Allen and go along with me,
> And I will make you Governor of Ohio's fair countrie.

The seventy-year-old Allen astonished his friends and foes by his vigorous campaign. In vitriolic language he attacked the Grant administration for rasing the taxes and "busying itself in making special laws for the benefit of corporations, cliques, and rings." "Defalcations," declared Allen, "is a soft word which means in plain English stealing." Allen won by a majority of 817 over his opponent, Governor Edward F. Noyes.

Governor Allen took his duties seriously. He rose early in the morning, breakfasted with his family, and by nine-thirty was in his executive offices. He conscientiously examined every official document before it received his signature. His health improved and he seemed to enjoy his work. In his messages to the legislature he stressed the need for economy, lower taxes, and the enforcement of the laws. In 1874, at his suggestion, more than 400,000 dollars were saved in the state's expenditures; and in 1875 the tax levy was reduced, thereby saving to the people more than 1,000,000 dollars.

The governor's appointments met with general approval, particularly his appointment of a practical miner as inspector of mines. The governor did not hesitate to call out the state militia to check disorders in Tuscarawas and Miami counties caused by a dispute between railroad officials and employees. He threatened to use troops in a coal dispute in the Hocking Valley region. The governor strove to regulate rather than coerce big business. He believed that the rights of property should be protected by law, but that the law must be respected.

Governor Allen's conservative, economical administration attracted national attention. Despite his age, Allen might have achieved still higher honors if he had not become the champion of inflation. He became a crusader for greenbacks while his nephew, Senator Thurman, stood for hard money. With dissension in the Democratic ranks, the Republican sound-money candidate, Rutherford B. Hayes, with the help of Carl Schurz and other national Republican leaders, defeated "old Bill Allen" in the heated "rag-baby" election of 1875. Allen again retired to private life, and on July 11, 1879, he died at his home, Fruit Hill, Chillicothe, survived by his daughter.

William Allen was a man of striking personal appearance and an effective, fluent speaker with a voice like a foghorn. He was a fiery partisan and a vigorous exponent of what he believed were the aspirations and rights of his section and his country. He was an old-fashioned Jacksonian Democrat of unquestioned integrity who found it difficult to cope with new issues as they arose. Today his statue by the sculptor Charles H. Niehaus stands in Statuary Hall, across from that of James A. Garfield, in the national capitol, as one of Ohio's distinguished representatives.

University of Cincinnati   REGINALD C. MCGRANE

THOMAS L. YOUNG
1877 - 1878

Rutherford B. Hayes resigned as governor of Ohio, effective March 2, 1877, to become the nineteenth president of the United States, and Lieutenant Governor Thomas Lowry Young of Cincinnati, who had served in both houses of the state legislature, was sworn in as governor for the unexpired term.

Most of the duties faced by Governor Young were routine, but a few months after taking office, he was confronted by a very serious labor situation in Ohio. This involved rioting and unrest as the result of a railroad strike beginning in Pennsylvania on July 22 and spreading rapidly to other states. At places in Pennsylvania and Maryland, riotous mobs destroyed many millions of dollars worth of property, and lives were lost in clashes with police and militia. In Ohio, at points along the lines of the Pennsylvania and the Baltimore and Ohio railroads, there was considerable tension and some disorder, with apprehension of disaster. Governor Young did not call upon the president of the United States for aid as did the governors of other states, but took personal charge of the situation and ordered the state militia into active service to maintain order. When asked why he did not turn to the president for assistance, he retorted, it is said, "Ohio can take care of herself." He would not appeal, he said, "until the last man in Ohio is whipped." The result of his timely action averted loss of life and property damage, and by early August peace had returned and the troops were disbanded.

Young was not a native of Ohio nor of the United States. He was born on December 14, 1832, in Killyleagh, County Down, on the estate of Lord Dufferin in the North of Ireland. At the age of twelve he immigrated to the United States with his parents, and was educated in the public schools of New York City. In 1848, near the close of the Mexican War, he enlisted in the United States Army as a musician and served ten years, advancing through the ranks from private to first sergeant. He left the army in January 1858, and a year later settled in Cincinnati to become an instructor and assistant superintendent of the House of Refuge Reform School for youth.

Three weeks before the bombardment of Fort Sumter, when civil war seemed to him to be inevitable, Young offered his services to General Winfield Scott, whom he knew personally, to organize volunteer forces for the United States government. But General Scott declined, believing his services would not be required. Between September and December 1861, after war broke out, he was captain of the Benton Cadets, Missouri Volunteers, said to have been General John C. Frémont's bodyguard. The next few months he spent in a somewhat aimless manner, part of the time editing a Democratic newspaper at Sidney, Ohio. As editor, he condemned the indecisive policy of those in charge of the conduct of the war and urged its vigorous prosecution.

But he could not be content with fighting the war on paper. In August 1862 he was commissioned major of the 118th Regiment, Ohio Volunteer Infantry, which was mustered into federal service the following month. For several weeks thereafter he was on detached service as provost marshal at various points in Kentucky. He was promoted, April 17, 1863, to lieutenant colonel and commanded his regiment in the East Tennessee campaign.

Young received his commission as colonel on April 11, 1864, and he spent the following month engaged in heavy fighting in Georgia. For courage and gallantry during the battle of Resaca, near Dalton,

Georgia, he was breveted brigadier general of volunteers. The hardships and disease of the campaign proved too much for him, and he was honorably discharged for disability in the fall of 1864.

Returning to Cincinnati, Young studied law and was admitted to practice in April 1865. In the same month he was appointed assistant city auditor of Cincinnati, and in the fall elections he was sent to the state house of representatives from Hamilton County for one term. Other positions of public trust came to him. He was elected recorder of Hamilton County in 1867, and the following year received an appointment from President Andrew Johnson as supervisor of internal revenue for the southern district of Ohio. Finding the duties of this position unpleasant under the Johnson administration, he resigned at the end of one year.

Next he was engaged in real estate activities for some months in 1870 with Daniel Weber and E. W. Langdon, but entered politics again in 1871 and was the only Republican elected to the state senate from Hamilton County that year. Completing the term as senator, Young turned to the private practice of law in Cincinnati with his partners, Ransford Smith and Samuel T. Crawford. His absence from public life was of short duration, however, for in the campaign of 1875 the Republican party nominated him for lieutenant governor to run on the ticket with Rutherford B. Hayes. Both were elected, and when Hayes later went to Washington as president, Young became governor of Ohio for slightly less than a year.

Young's last venture in politics was to serve as a representative from the Cincinnati district in the 46th and 47th congresses, 1879-83. He was defeated for renomination for a third term, and thereupon withdrew from politics to resume the private practice of law. He died in Cincinnati on July 20, 1888, and was buried in Spring Grove Cemetery. Young had been married three times, and was survived by eight children.

The Hayes Memorial Library   Watt P. Marchman

RICHARD M. BISHOP
1878 - 1880

At the close of the Mexican War in 1848, Richard Moore Bishop arrived in Cincinnati from Mount Sterling, Kentucky. He was thirty-six years old at the time, having been born November 4, 1812, in Fleming County, Kentucky, of English and German stock. His parents had immigrated to the western country from Virginia in 1800, and Richard grew up with the limited schooling available on the frontier. At the age of seventeen he began his business career as clerk in a country store and became a partner in the store at the end of four years.

During the period 1838 to 1841 he and his brother carried on a pork business in Fleming County, shipping down river to the southern trade. This proved to be an unfortunate enterprise and ended in failure when prices collapsed and banks in Mississippi suspended payment. The brothers, however, soon resumed business and continued their partnership until Richard removed to Cincinnati and established the wholesale grocery firm of Bishop, Wells and Company. Subsequently, in partnership with his three sons under the name of R. M. Bishop and Company, Bishop developed the firm till it boasted a sales volume of five million dollars a year.

Bishop's political career, which eventually was to make him governor of Ohio, began in Cincinnati in 1857. At that time he was elected a member of the city council from the second ward by a large majority, and was thereafter presiding officer of that body. In 1859, during the times of trouble preceding the Civil War, he was elected mayor of Cincinnati and continued in that office until 1861. Bishop's popularity as mayor is attested by the fact that both parties offered him the nomination at the end of his term. He declined the offer and temporarily retired to private life.

Two events of considerable national interest took place in Cincinnati while Bishop was mayor. On Friday, January 27, 1860, a time when threats of secession were in the air, the legislators and other representative citizens of Kentucky, Tennessee, Indiana, and Ohio gathered in the city to promote friendship and unity between the states. At a grand reception at Pike's Opera House, Mayor Bishop welcomed the visitors to the western metropolis, and Judge Bellamy Storer, as principal orator, spoke for the Union.

In February of the following year, on the brink of war, Lincoln passed through Cincinnati on the way to his inauguration, and Mayor Bishop had the distinction of welcoming him to the city.

It is said that the laws were rigidly enforced during Bishop's administration, and that Sabbath desecration in various forms was suppressed in the city. His strict attitude in regard to such offenses reflected his early training and church affiliation. Bishop joined the Baptist Church at the age of sixteen and, like his family, was a follower of Alexander Campbell into the so-called "Campbellite heresy." Thereafter he joined the Church of the Disciples (the Christian Church), and continued a faithful and prominent member of that denomination, actually succeeding Alexander Campbell as president of the General Christian Missionary Convention.

Both before and after his term as governor of Ohio, Bishop held offices in the world of education, business, and politics. He was a curator of Bethany College, Virginia, president of the board of curators of the University of Kentucky, and a trustee of McMicken University, now the University of Cincinnati. Banking and insurance, in addition to wholesale groceries, were included in his business interests. He was a member of the board of directors of the First National Bank of Cincinnati.

In 1867 Bishop was living on the northeast corner of Eighth and Mound streets, Cincinnati, where he spent "much of his time beautifying the splendid grounds around his house." The West End in the Mound Street area was then the fashionable part of the city; today it is a fit subject for extensive rehabilitation.

At that period in his life Bishop was supposed to have retired from politics according to one source: "His name has been prominent among those from whom the nominee to the gubernatorial chair was to be selected. But he is not a politician, cares not for office, and has never accepted one unless at the urgent request and unanimous wishes of the mercantile community of which he is a representative member. His high-toned ideas of right and truth, and his inflexible honesty will ever prevent his appearance in political circles."

Six years later, however, Bishop was elected one of forty-six Democratic delegates to the Ohio Constitutional Convention, there being in addition fifty Republicans and nine Liberals or Independents. This convention met on May 14, 1873, in Columbus and ended its long deliberations finally at the Spencer House in Cincinnati in May 1874. Thus the reluctant candidate was drawn back into politics, and three years later, in 1877, found himself elected governor of the state over Judge William H. West of Bellefontaine. As a businessman, bank director, and trustee of the Southern Railroad, Bishop, at the age of sixty-five, was relatively conservative and had, therefore, attracted many Republican votes from his outspoken and liberal opponent. With the exception of William Allen he was at that time the only Democrat elected to the governor's office since 1856.

Bishop had campaigned against the Resumption Act of 1875 by which the federal government resumed specie payment on legal tender notes, and he had also favored the remonetization of silver. Under his leadership the general assembly passed joint resolutions condemning the Resumption Act and approving the Bland-Allison Act which provided for the coinage of silver.

During the Bishop administration there was little significant legislation passed. Codification of the laws of the state, started in preceding administrations, was continued. Bribery in elections was made a serious offense, and blackmail was defined and made punishable by a prison term of one to five years and a fine of up to one thousand dollars. The state penal and welfare institutions were reorganized and put in the hands of Democrats.

The general assembly was dubbed the "O'Connor Legislature" during these years. John O'Connor, a Republican representative from Montgomery County, it was found, was a Civil War deserter and former penitentiary convict in Michigan. After investigation, his seat was declared vacant.

Bishop's administration was satisfactory without being impressive for accomplishments. Leaders of the party, however, were disgruntled by the influence one of the governor's sons had exercised in making political appointments. Bishop was shunted aside, therefore, by the state Democratic convention of 1879, which nominated Thomas Ewing, Jr., of Lancaster for governor. The Democrats, weakened by strife within the party, lost the election. At the end of his tenure Bishop retired from public life and resumed his private activities in Cincinnati. He died in Jacksonville, Florida, on March 2, 1893.

The Historical and Philosophical Society of Ohio   VIRGINIUS C. HALL

CHARLES FOSTER
1880 - 1884

Charles Foster (April 12, 1828–January 9, 1904) was a businessman and the son of a businessman, Charles W. Foster. As chief executive of Ohio, 1880-84, he was a businessman governor. His years as secretary of the treasury, 1891-93, under President Benjamin Harrison fitted into the same pattern.

Foster learned his business ways with his father, a pioneer land-owner in Seneca County, who in 1832 in Rome set up his double log cabin which combined home and store. This store became one of the chief mercantile and credit institutions of this area of Ohio. Periodically the "Foster wagon train," loaded with farmers' grain, crossed the Black Swamp to Perrysburg where it picked up the merchandise used to stock the Foster store. When Rome and adjacent Risdon combined in 1854, it was a tribute to the influence of the Foster store that the new town was called Fostoria.

Six years before that date, young Foster, aged eighteen, had become his father's partner. At the age of nineteen the young man assumed full charge. And in 1853 he added to his responsibilities by marrying Ann M. Olmsted, by whom he had two daughters. It was not surprising, therefore, that, when the Civil War came along, it was essential for him to remain in business. During the conflict he aided in recruiting and followed the policy of giving extended credit to needy families of soldiers. After the war, political opponents dubbed him "Calico Charlie" because of his preference for a mercantile career over a military one. He and his friends, however, transformed this into a term of endearment rather than one of opprobrium.

During these years Charles Foster established a wide reputation in northwestern Ohio for probity and enterprise. This helps to account for his elevation to public life, which began in 1870 with the first of four consecutive elections to congress as a Republican. In congress his constructive and conservative participation in legislation gained him further renown. As a member of the ways and means committee he took a determined part in exposing frauds in the treasury department growing out of the policy of farming out uncollected taxes at fifty percent commission to J. D. Sanborn, a political henchman of Ben Butler of Massachusetts. Foster was strong in curbing radical Republican interests in southern reconstruction. In the Louisiana contested election of 1874 he voted against the Radical Republicans, and in the contested national election of 1876 he was a spokesman for his friend and neighbor, Rutherford B. Hayes, in assuring southerners that Hayes' election to the presidency would lead to the withdrawal of federal troops from the South.

The way was prepared for his entry into state politics in Ohio by his defeat for reelection to congress in 1878, presumably brought about by a Democratic gerrymander. Sound money was the issue in the state election of 1879, and Foster supported the policy of gold redemption of the paper money currency called greenbacks. He had been firm in the support of this policy in congress. Running for governor on the sound-money platform, he was elected and in his two terms in this office did much to inject business methods into state financial affairs. Among his contributions were the establishment of bi-partisan boards to manage public institutions, the promotion of effective mine inspection, the introduction of adequate forest protection measures, and the revision of the tax system. He became involved in the temperance issue by favoring rather high taxation of liquor, a stand which contributed to his defeat for reelection in 1883.

This defeat damaged his prestige as a leader in the Republican party, though he did remain influential in party councils. His ability to analyze voting records and his accuracy in predicting election results won him the title of "Old Figgers, Jr." In 1891 Foster returned to a position of leadership in the Republican party when President Harrison made him secretary of the treasury. In this office he became involved in the question of the free coinage of silver by the federal government. This he considered too inflationary, although he supported the partial coinage of new silver as provided in the Sherman Silver Purchase Act of 1890. He remained loyal, however, to the principles of sound money by administering the coinage so as to maintain the parity of gold and silver. He was in favor of greater issues of silver (bimetallism) only if handled on an international basis.

Meanwhile, Foster had continued to develop his business interests. He invested in railroads, oil, mining, rubber, and other corporate ventures. In the late 1880's he was president of the Northwestern Ohio Natural Gas Company, a Standard Oil subsidiary, which came into conflict with the city of Toledo's efforts to set up a publicly-owned natural gas enterprise. He became deeply interested in the State Hospital for the Insane at Toledo of which he was board president for many years. Under his influence the "cottage system" was first inaugurated and later strengthened. This institution became widely known for its progressive methods of treatment of mental illness.

The Historical Society of Northwestern Ohio   RANDOLPH C. DOWNES

GEORGE HOADLY
1884 - 1886

Like many of Ohio's statesmen who antedated him, George Hoadly, the state's thirty-sixth governor, was a native of Connecticut. He was born at New Haven on July 31, 1826, to parents of notable lineage. His father was George Hoadly, Yale graduate and one-time mayor of New Haven, and his mother was Mary Ann Woolsey, a granddaughter of Timothy Dwight and a great-granddaughter of Jonathan Edwards.

The family moved to Cleveland around 1830. After attending the public schools there until he was fourteen, George enrolled at Western Reserve College at Hudson. Having determined to enter the legal profession, he studied law at Harvard for a year under the tutelage of Professors Story and Greenleaf, spent another year in the office of Charles C. Converse, a prominent Zanesville attorney who was later a state supreme court justice, and in 1846 became associated with Salmon P. Chase and his partner at Cincinnati. Upon being admitted to the bar a year later, the young lawyer was accepted as a partner in the firm, the name of which was then expanded to Chase, Ball, and Hoadly.

The absence of Chase, who was elected to the United States Senate in 1849, enabled Hoadly to appear in many important court cases. The prestige accruing from these appearances had its effect on the legislature, which in 1851 elected him judge of the superior court at Cincinnati. Four years later he became city solicitor.

In 1856 Chase, who had won the gubernatorial election of the preceding year, offered Hoadly a seat on the state supreme court. He declined the appointment, however, as he did six years later when Governor Tod made a similar proposal. Giving up the solicitorship in 1859, Hoadly again was elected judge of the superior court to succeed William Y. Gholson. His victory was repeated five years later, but in 1866 he resigned and established the legal firm of Hoadly, Jackson, and Johnson. He had become a member of the Cincinnati Law School faculty in 1864, commencing an affiliation which lasted, with interruptions, for twenty-three years. During part of this time he was also a trustee of the University of Cincinnati.

Hoadly in his early years was a Democrat, but the series of events leading up to the Civil War led him into the young Republican party. It would have been surprising had he not taken a stand against slavery, in view of his relationship with Chase. The Republican party held him only as long as slavery was the paramount issue. Disgruntled over the reconstruction policy of the party, Hoadly sought satisfaction in the Liberal Republican movement. Here, too, disillusionment was not long in coming, for the choice of the 1872 convention, Horace Greeley, was unpalatable to him.

Reluctantly he supported Grant for reelection, as the lesser of evils, but the Republican tariff policy effectively alienated him from the party itself. Soon, although he frowned on Greenbackism, Hoadly returned to the Democratic fold after an absence of some twenty years. The high regard felt for him by party leaders was evinced by their request that he serve as counsel for Tilden in the dispute following the presidential election of 1876. He complied and presented the claims of the Oregon and Florida electors before the electoral commission. In 1880 he was chosen temporary chairman of the Democratic national convention.

As the gubernatorial election of 1883 approached, Hoadly threw his hat into the ring. The only other serious contender for the Democratic nomination was General Durbin Ward of Lebanon. The victory-hungry Democrats—they had been in power only twice in over twenty years—

wanted a man who could provide an efficient administration and at the same time deal skillfully with the delicate liquor problem. Both candidates had strong backing, but when on the second round of voting in the convention Hoadly lengthened his first-ballot lead, the Ward forces capitulated.

The hopes of the Republicans were riding on another Cincinnatian, Joseph B. Foraker, a rapidly-rising young man who was little known outside his home town. Illness curtailed Hoadly's campaign activities, but the Republican-dominated general assembly had made his task easier by passing a law taxing all places where liquor was sold at retail and forbidding its sale on Sunday. This alienated a considerable segment of the population, including large numbers of German Republicans, who either crossed the party lines or stayed away from the polls. Judge Hoadly received nearly 360,000 votes, some 12,500 more than his opponent, and carried along with him a Democratic majority in the legislature.

Several incidents which occurred during his term as governor caused Hoadly to lose some of his prestige and popularity. Two of these involved the use of the state militia to quell disturbances early in 1884. In March Cincinnatians, already disturbed over the prevalence of crime in their city, rose in resentment when a cold-blooded murderer was convicted only of manslaughter. A large crowd marched on the jail with the intention of hanging the offender and was so incensed at learning that he was already en route to Columbus for imprisonment that it burned the courthouse, destroying valuable records and precipitating street fighting which claimed a number of lives. Pursuing his belief that troops should be employed only as a last resort, Governor Hoadly did not call out the militia to restore order until this course was urgently advocated by a member of his military staff. The long delay inspired much criticism of the governor.

Public opinion was further aroused in the next month when Hoadly dispatched troops to the scene of disturbances resulting from a coal miners' strike in the Hocking Valley. The more conservative element of the electorate again felt that he should have acted more quickly, while labor sympathizers resented the use of the militia at all.

An Ohio political scandal which reacted more against the Democratic party than against Hoadly himself caught the attention of the nation in 1884. The controversy centered upon the election of a United

States Senator by the general assembly. George H. Pendleton, the incumbent, desired reelection, but his candidacy was oppossed by Durbin Ward and Henry B. Payne, a 73-year-old Cleveland millionaire. All three were Democrats as was the majority in the legislature at the time. Ward's early elimination resulted in a bitter struggle between the adherents of Payne and Pendleton, with the former emerging victorious. It was widely and openly charged that the Standard Oil Company, through its treasurer who was Payne's son, bought the votes of many of the Democratic legislators. The succeeding Republican-controlled general assembly conducted an investigation, but the United States Senate, to which the evidence was submitted, refused to take any action against Payne.

In the summer of 1884 Governor Hoadly's dreams of higher honors began to crumble around him. As head of an important pivotal state, he had cause to hope for the Democratic presidential nomination. His name was placed before the convention, but whatever chance he may have had was lessened by the presence in the race of another aspiring Ohioan, Allen G. Thurman, and the coveted prize went to Grover Cleveland of New York. Although successful in his quest for renomination for governor in 1885, Hoadly was destined for further disappointment. A series of public debates in which he and his opponent, again Joseph B. Foraker, engaged failed to erase from the minds of the electorate the more unsavory aspects of his administration and Hoadly went down to defeat by a margin of some 17,000 votes.

Thoroughly disgusted, the erstwhile governor renounced politics, in which he had never been very adept, and returned to the practice of law, where he excelled. Although offered a cabinet post by his friend Cleveland during his second term, Hoadly declined, preferring not to reenter public life. Removing to New York in 1887, he established the firm of Hoadly, Lauterbach, and Johnson. They were leading corporation lawyers and handled such important litigations as the Jefferson Davis estate's and Mrs. Davis' suit against the Bedford Publishing Company.

Before he left Cincinnati Hoadly voluntarily paid $50,000 when a man for whom he had signed bond defaulted. This left him a comparatively poor man, but in fifteen years in New York he more than recouped his wealth. During the summer of 1902 he contracted acute bronchitis and died on August 26. Mary Burnet Perry Hoadly, granddaughter of the notable early Cincinnatian, Jacob Burnet, and Hoadly's wife for fifty-one years, outlived him by a year. He was also survived by two sons and a daughter.

The Ohio Historical Society JOHN S. STILL

JOSEPH B. FORAKER
1886 - 1890

Joseph Benson Foraker, thirty-seventh governor of Ohio, was born July 5, 1846, near Rainsboro, Highland County, Ohio. His ancestors were English and Scotch-Irish; his paternal grandfather, John Fouracre, had emigrated from Devonshire, England, in the early eighteenth century and had settled in Delaware. Foraker's parents, Henry Stacey and Margaret (Reece) Foraker, were early Ohio settlers. Young "Ben," as he was called during his youth, was a typical Ohio farm lad, helping with the chores, fishing and swimming, and putting in a few months at school each year. He attended Sunday School and church services at the Methodist Episcopal church. When only sixteen years old he enlisted in Company "A," 89th Regiment, Ohio Volunteer Infantry, and with this unit saw action in West Virginia and Tennessee. In 1864, as a lieutenant under General William T. Sherman, he marched through Georgia to the sea, and in 1865 through the Carolinas and Virginia. He was mustered out a captain in June 1865.

120

As a farm boy he had made up his mind to become a lawyer, and upon his return to civilian life he set out to enter that profession. To this end he attended Salem Academy, Ohio Wesleyan University, and Cornell University; he was graduated a member of the first class of Cornell in 1869. That same year he was admitted to the Cincinnati bar, and soon thereafter became a successful attorney.

To confirm his legal reputation he ran for and was elected judge of the superior court of Cincinnati for the term 1879-81. His judicious conduct on the bench as well as his oratorical skill at political gatherings attracted the attention of Ohio Republican leaders who, in 1883, persuaded him to run for governor. Although unable to overcome the unfavorable position of his party that year, he did become acquainted with important Republicans. Two years later he defeated George Hoadly, the Democratic gubernatorial candidate.

Foraker served capably as governor for two terms. Limited in his executive powers by the Ohio constitution, he was able to bring about only part of the reforms he advocated. In an attempt to clean up the abysmal election practices, he was successful in sponsoring laws requiring the registration of voters and the formation of nonpartisan election boards in the state's larger cities. To meet the impending deficit created by the excessive spending of the preceding administration, Foraker proposed numerous measures to increase state revenues. Of these only the Dow Law, regulating the sale of and taxing intoxicating beverages, was enacted by a spendthrift but tax-shy legislature.

The unrealistic attitude of the general assembly on finances forced Foraker to refund the state debt on his own initiative, a measure of leadership which won him wide acclaim. After extensive investigation of Cincinnati's corrupt police force and public works administration, he appointed boards to bring about much needed reforms. At his urging, the legislature in 1886 created a state board of health and a board of managers to govern the state penitentiary. His second term was marked by celebrations at Marietta, Cincinnati, and Columbus of the centennial of the beginnings of organized settlement in the Northwest Territory. His attempt for a third term was unsuccessful.

Although a strong Republican, he played the "lone wolf" in Ohio politics. His faction, the "young Republicans," in the eighties and early nineties steadfastly and openly opposed the Sherman-Hanna-McKinley group. This opposition caused him to be accused in 1884 and 1888 of attempting to obtain the Republican presidential nomination for himself. In 1892 his independence led him to contest the venerable John Sherman for the senatorship. After this unsuccessful campaign, he quietly built up a state-wide organization and won election to the senate in 1896. His election was assured in 1895 at the Zanesville convention, which was controlled by the masterfully organized Foraker forces. Much of his political strength stemmed from the consistent support of "Boss" Cox of Cincinnati.

During the 1880's he was a leader in the use of the "Bloody Shirt" in campaigns. Early in his political career he had learned that his audiences throve on Civil War issues, and as he later stated, "I gave them what they wanted." His colorful mannerisms and trenchant verbal thrusts won him the sobriquet, "Fire Alarm Foraker." Later he quieted down, becoming one of the foremost speakers in the Midwest and East. While governor, his uncompromising Republicanism led him to bait President Cleveland. In reply to the latter's request to return to the South captured Confederate battle flags then in various state capitols, Foraker publicly announced, "No rebel flags will be surrendered while I am governor."

During the McKinley administration Foraker was known as an "administration senator." He took a position of leadership on our entry into the Spanish-American War and in the wave of imperialism which followed. As chairman of the committee on the Pacific islands and Puerto Rico, he sponsored and pushed through to adoption the Foraker Act, the organic law for the recently-acquired island of Puerto Rico. He also served on the powerful foreign relations committee of the senate.

A representative of the conservatives, Foraker did not go along with Theodore Roosevelt's "Square Deal" and its efforts to achieve social justice. His opposition reached its climax over the Hepburn Bill of 1906 which was designed to regulate railroads. He was the only Republican senator to vote against it. His opposition to Roosevelt developed into open battle during the complex Brownsville case in which Foraker took the part of a Negro regiment summarily discharged by a hasty and ill-considered presidential order.

As a result of the publication of the Archbold-Foraker letters he was retired from politics in 1908. These letters, published by William Randolph Hearst, disclosed that during his first term as senator Foraker had been employed as special counsel for the Standard Oil Company of

Ohio. The relationship with business, not uncommon in the preceding era, was considered unethical by the nation in 1908.

After his political retirement he continued his law practice in Cincinnati, representing many large corporations. In 1914 he was, as he later stated, "wheedled" into the senatorial primary to run against Warren G. Harding, for years a staunch Forakerite. The younger man won both the primary and the election. During his last years Foraker relived his eventful life while writing his autobiography, *Notes of a Busy Life*. He died on May 10, 1917.

An interesting memoir of Foraker and his period is *I Would Live It Again*, written by his wife and the mother of his five children, Julia Bundy Foraker.

The Ohio State University   EVERETT WALTERS

JAMES E. CAMPBELL
1890 - 1892

The thirty-eighth governor of Ohio, James Edwin Campbell, was the first Ohio governor whose parents were both natives of the Buckeye state. Governor Campbell was proud to be what he called the first specimen of the "second growth of timber." He was born in Middletown, Ohio, on July 7, 1843, the son of Laura Reynolds and Andrew Campbell, a successful surgeon.

James attended the public schools of his home town and studied privately with the pastor of the Middletown Presbyterian Church. Later, he read law and taught school.

In the summer of 1863 he enlisted in the United States Navy and served in the Mississippi and Red River flotillas. He contracted break-bone fever, however, and was discharged from the service.

As soon as his health permitted it, he resumed the study of law. He was admitted to the bar in 1865, and in 1867 began the practice of law in Hamilton, Ohio. He was elected prosecuting attorney of

Butler County in 1875 and 1877. Meanwhile in 1870, he had married Libby Owens. The Campbells had four children.

Campbell was a Republican until 1872, when he voted for Horace Greeley, the Liberal Republican candidate for president. After that he became and remained a staunch Democrat. In 1882, 1884, and 1886, he was elected to congress, winning his seat in 1886 by only two votes.

In 1889 Campbell ran against Joseph Benson Foraker for the governorship. The Republican party was strongly entrenched, and "Fighting Joe" was a formidable opponent. But "Jimmie" Campbell had an amazing capacity for hard work and organizational detail. Murat Halstead, noted publisher of the *Cincinnati Commercial Gazette,* bitterly opposing him, said that Campbell would drive across three counties on a rainy night to clinch a single vote.

The slogan of the campaign was "Home Rule for the Cities of Ohio." To the lively tune of "The Campbells Are Coming," great crowds turned out to hear the man that could give "Fire Alarm" Foraker measure for measure in ridicule and invective. Foraker was running for a third term. Campbell denounced the third term as a bad precedent, charged corruption in state institutions, and boldly advocated home rule. His sensational exposure of one of Governor Foraker's graft-practicing appointees to the Cincinnati Board of Control was a staggering blow to the Republicans. To counteract this scandal, Murat Halstead, unwisely and without Foraker's consent, published what he thought was the genuine signature of Campbell to a contract for a financial interest in a ballot box. The signature was a forgery, and Halstead was forced to publish a retraction of the famous ballot-box hoax. The campaign grew hotter and hotter and Campbell drove himself harder and harder, and defeated Foraker by 10,872 votes.

In his inaugural address Governor Campbell insisted that the governor of Ohio should be divested of authority to appoint election boards and clerks and various other governing boards which enabled him virtually to control most of the cities. The general assembly acted on his advice in some cases, but refused to follow him in the case of Cincinnati's board of public affairs which had complete jurisdiction over the city. Greatly chagrined, Governor Campbell had to appoint the members of the Cincinnati board. Soon he had reason to suspect the integrity of some of those appointees. He called a special session of the general assembly and demanded that they fulfill the promises of the

Democratic party. After much wrangling, the general assembly passed "the ripper bill" which restored to the mayor of Cincinnati the right to appoint the board of public affairs. Governor Campbell knew that he was committing political suicide, for the president of the Cincinnati Board of Public Affairs was also the chairman of the Democratic committee of Hamilton County.

The general assembly of 1890-91 enacted important labor laws. By that time workers' unions were politically potent. In April 1890 the legislature authorized union labels on union-made goods, established free employment agencies in most of the cities of Ohio, and designated the first Monday in September as Labor Day. Ohio was among the first states to recognize Labor Day as a legal holiday. All corporations were ordered to pay their employees at least twice a month. Railroad companies were obliged to pay a higher rate for labor performed beyond the ten-hour day. Those companies could no longer compel their employees to sign agreements which relieved the employers of all responsibility for injuries incurred by the employees while at work. It was a well-known fact that fifty-six percent of all accidents to railroad employees occurred in coupling cars. On April 24, 1891, the general assembly declared itself in favor of a national law requiring railroad companies to install automatic couplers on all cars.

The crowning achievement of Governor Campbell's administration was the introduction of the Australian ballot system in elections by an act passed on April 30, 1891. At that time only two or three states were using the Australian ballot. Braver than his predecessors, Govenor Campbell also recommended a permanent levy on the tax duplicate for the benefit of the Ohio State University. To his great surprise and gratification, it passed without opposition.

Governor Campbell was renominated in 1891, but he was defeated by William McKinley. It was a hard-fought campaign, but a clean one. McKinley and Campbell were warm friends. Throughout the campaign they were known as "two gentlemen in politics." It was generally recognized that the real stake was the presidency. Had Campbell won, he might have succeeded Benjamin Harrison as president of the United States.

Much against his wishes, the Democratic state convention nominated Campbell for governor again in 1895. He was certain that he faced defeat, because the tide was still running against the Democrats. His acceptance speech contained fourteen words: "A good soldier may fall, but he dare not falter. I accept the nomination." Though he put up the hardest fight of his career, he was defeated by Asa S. Bushnell.

From 1907 to 1910 Governor Campbell was a member of the commission to revise and codify the statutes of Ohio. He practiced law in Columbus for a time and later had business interests in New York City. He never changed his legal residence, however, from Butler County, the "Democratic Gibraltar."

Campbell was an able lawyer, a skillful politician, and a thorough student of the history of his state. He contributed much to the growth of the Ohio Historical Society, and was president of that organization when he died on December 17, 1924.

Oxford, Ohio   OPHIA D. SMITH

WILLIAM McKINLEY
1892 - 1896

Ohio's thirty-ninth governor and the twenty-fifth president of the United States, William McKinley, symbolized the passing of nineteenth-century America. Typical of his era, he stood fast for certain post-Civil War beliefs during his career as congressman and governor and for four years as president. But in the last year of his presidency he came to recognize, as did many Americans, that the isolationism of the country was breaking down and that Americans must come to play a larger role in world affairs. So, too, he came to sense the deep maladjustment of American life and the dominance of powerful business interests.

McKinley was born at Niles, Ohio, January 29, 1843, the seventh son of William and Nancy Allison McKinley. His ancestors on both sides were Scotch, Scotch-Irish, and English; his American ancestors settled in central Pennsylvania during the eighteenth century. The McKinley family in Pennsylvania and later in Ohio was engaged in the manufacture of iron. William McKinley, Sr., operated a small pig-iron furnace in Niles.

Because of poor school facilities in Niles, the McKinley family moved to Poland, although McKinley's father continued his work in Niles. During his boyhood years McKinley attended the local school and Poland Seminary. At the age of ten, during the religious fervor of a revival meeting, he joined the Methodist Church.

At seventeen he entered Allegheny College, Meadville, Pennsylvania, but returned after a short time because of ill health. Family financial reverses prevented resumption of his college studies, and in 1861 he took a job teaching school. Caught up in the excitement of the Civil War, he enlisted on June 11, 1861, in Company "E," 23d Ohio Volunteer Infantry, a unit noted for its distinguished leaders, William S. Rosecrans, Stanley Matthews, and Rutherford B. Hayes. With the 23d, in 1862 he saw extensive action in West Virginia, then at Antietam; in 1864 he fought in Virginia in the campaign to halt the Confederate army under General Jubal Early. In the summer of 1864 he was appointed to General George Crook's staff. At war's end he was made a brevet major and was mustered out on July 26, 1865.

Soon after his release from the army he began the study of law, first in Poland and then for a time at the Albany Law School. In 1867 he was admitted to the bar and set up practice in Canton. As a lawyer he won a reputation for stating issues clearly and forcibly and for honesty before the bar. Meanwhile, he had taken an interest in politics, making speeches in the Canton area for his old commander, Rutherford Hayes, then running for governor.

In 1869 McKinley was elected prosecuting attorney of Stark County. Seven years later he was elected congressman from the eighteenth district of Ohio. Despite constant gerrymandering of this district, he served as congressman from 1876 to 1890, with the exception of the period from May 27, 1884, to March 3, 1885, when he was unseated in a contested election by Jonathan H. Wallace.

In congress McKinley became a leading exponent of protection. Through hours of study he came to possess a thorough knowledge of American industry and was able to contest sharply the Democrats who labored for a lower tariff, especially in 1884 and 1888. Such was his political stature by 1889 that he was able to compete with Thomas B. Reed for speaker of the house. He lost the contest but was rewarded by the appointment as chairman of the powerful ways and means committee. In this capacity he championed a new tariff bill which became law in 1890 and bore his name. Although he first voted for the Bland Bill to promote silver coinage, he later became a staunch adherent of "sound" money.

Following his defeat for congressman in 1890, he returned to private life, but was persuaded to run for governor in 1891. He was easily elected. By this time he had received support of the Sherman-Hanna faction of the Republican party. Major McKinley, as he was familiarly called, was a popular speaker in Ohio and the Midwest. His honesty, dignity, and kindly manner won him thousands of loyal followers. He served as an Ohio delegate at the Republican national conventions in 1884, 1888, and 1892; at the latter two he received powerful support as a dark horse.

As governor McKinley developed a new and more comprehensive tax system which, by levying excise taxes on corporations, aided in the reduction of the state debt. At his insistence legislation was enacted which required installation of certain safety devices on railroads. During the industrial strife of the nineties he introduced and promoted the enactment of a law which set up a state board of arbitration. This board settled numerous labor disputes but failed to prevent the serious coal strike of 1894. At the height of the strike McKinley called out the national guard to prevent the destruction of private property in several strike-bound counties. That same year he used the guard to put down a series of lynchings. In 1895 he organized private groups to aid in rendering assistance to the suffering unemployed coal miners in the Hocking Valley.

Soon after McKinley's reelection as governor, he became the leading contender for the Republican presidential nomination. Mark Hanna retired from his prosperous coal and iron business to manage the major's campaign. McKinley easily won the nomination at the 1896 convention at St. Louis. During the campaign, one of the most memorable in the nation's history, he remained at his Canton home, receiving delegations from various sections of the country and delivering to them carefully prepared "front porch speeches." This astute maneuver proved a dramatic contrast to the extensive whirlwind campaign tour of the brilliant Democratic candidate, William Jennings Bryan. McKinley won by well over a half million votes.

The first year of his presidency, 1897, was marked by the passage of the Dingley Tariff and the appointment of commissioners to the International Monetary Conference. In his second year the public interest in Cuba swelled to bursting, and following the historic *Maine* incident, McKinley asked congress to declare war on Spain. During the brief Spanish-American War, April to August 1898, he maintained direct control over the armed forces, making most of the important decisions himself.

Similarly, after the war, McKinley made the far-reaching decision to retain the Philippines and Puerto Rico, thus launching the United States upon the course of imperialism. In the first days of the war he had urged the annexation of Hawaii as the natural result of "manifest destiny." He also encouraged American interest in China, through the Open Door notes, and in world trade, through the exploration of possible routes for an isthmian canal.

The imperialistic policies proved popular with the American people who returned McKinley to office for a second term. His plans for reciprocal tariffs with foreign countries and for curbing the trusts were cut short only six months after his second inauguration by his untimely death. At the Buffalo Exposition, where he had delivered a speech on the significance of recent American progress and the prospects for the future, he was shot down by an assassin. He died on September 14, 1901, from complications resulting from his wounds. The American people mourned his death for they had come to revere him for his deep religious convictions, his devotion to his invalid wife, Ida, his dignity, and his kindliness. In 1904 the Ohio General Assembly adopted the red carnation, McKinley's favorite flower, as the state flower in honor of the martyred president.

The Ohio State University   EVERETT WALTERS

ASA S. BUSHNELL
1896 - 1900

Asa Smith Bushnell, governor of Ohio from 1896 to 1900, was a Springfield businessman who was identified with the Foraker wing of the Republican party. Born in 1834 into an old New England family in Rome, New York, he came to Ohio at the age of eleven. Bushnell's father, Daniel, was an active worker on the Underground Railroad, and a cousin, Simeon Bushnell, was imprisoned for his part in the Oberlin-Wellington rescue case. The future governor, however, seems to have been more interested in acquisitive enterprise than in antislavery agitation. He separated from his family at an early age, obtained a scant education in the public schools of Cincinnati, and, at seventeen, was supporting himself as a dry goods clerk in Springfield. Three years later he had risen to the more remunerative position of bookkeeper in a prominent business firm, and, following his marriage in 1857 to Miss Ellen Ludlow, he became a partner in his father-in-law's drug store.

Bushnell's business career was briefly interrupted in the summer of 1864, when he served as captain of a "hundred-day company" of infantry assigned to guard and picket duty in the Shenandoah Valley.

Several years after the war he acquired a partnership in a concern which manufactured reapers and mowers. At this time Springfield was a center of the agricultural implement industry. Bushnell's firm flourished, and his holding in it was the principal source of his large fortune. During his later years, he was president not only of the implement company but also of the First National Bank of Springfield and of the Springfield Gas Company. He was also prominently connected with the street railway and telephone companies of the city.

Bushnell's first important political assignment came in 1885 when, as chairman of the Republican state executive committee, he managed the successful gubernatorial campaign of Joseph Benson Foraker. His own nomination as Republican candidate for governor in 1895 was obtained through the support of Foraker and George B. Cox, the political boss of Cincinnati, and against the opposition of the forces of John Sherman and Mark Hanna. In the ensuing campaign Bushnell defeated his Democratic opponent, James E. Campbell, by over 90,000 votes.

The first order of business in Bushnell's administration was the election of Foraker to the United States Senate. Foraker's influence remained strong throughout both of Bushnell's terms as governor. In 1896 the senator-elect secured the passage by the Ohio General Assembly of the notorious Rogers Law which permitted Cincinnati officials to grant a fifty-year extension of its franchise to the Cincinnati Street Railway Company. Senator Foraker later represented the transit firm before Governor Bushnell and the state board of tax remission and succeeded in winning a $285,000 reduction in the company's tax valuation.

In 1897 the elevation of John Sherman from his seat in the United States Senate to the post of secretary of state in President McKinley's cabinet presented Bushnell with a difficult decision. It was the governor's responsibility to name the person to fill the unexpired portion of Sherman's term. Mark Hanna was an avowed and determined candidate for the appointment, but Bushnell, a Foraker adherent and a long-time foe of Hanna in the state organization, was reluctant to give him the commission. Nevertheless he realized that a break with the national administration would be politically inexpedient. He delayed naming Hanna as long as possible, yielding at last when both the president and Boss Cox had signified their desire to have the appointment go to Hanna.

At the Republican state convention in 1897 Bushnell was re-nominated, but, with the accession of Cox to the Hanna camp, the state party machinery passed to the control of Hanna. In the campaign of 1897 the election of a legislature which could be relied on to send the Clevelander to a full term in the senate seems to have been a more important goal of the party organization than the return of Bushnell to the statehouse. Bushnell was reelected, but by a much narrower margin of victory than in 1895. When the legislature assembled early in 1898, he supported the anti-Hanna group in a bitter but fruitless effort to prevent the election of Hanna to the senate.

Like Foraker and Secretary of War Russell A. Alger, with whom he was also on friendly terms, Bushnell was an advocate of intervention in Cuba. Even before the declaration of war with Spain in April 1898, he authorized the adjutant general to purchase sufficient stores of equipment to place Ohio's military establishment on a war footing; in the absence of legislative authorization for the expenditures, Bushnell gave his personal guarantee of payment for the purchases. He issued orders for the mobilization of the state's armed forces immediately upon receipt of the first presidential call and, in his annual message noted with pride that "Ohio was the first State in the Union to put a volunteer regiment in the field."

Despite or possibly because of the factional strife that characterized it, Bushnell's administration saw the enactment of legislation of considerable significance. Acting on the governor's recommendation, the general assembly adopted laws levying excise taxes on public utility companies and certain other corporations. The increased revenues obtained from these measures led to the further development of corporation taxation in succeeding administrations and to the eventual abandonment of the direct property tax as a source of revenue for the state government.

Bushnell's attorney general, Frank S. Monnett, renewed the legal attack on the Standard Oil Company which one of his predecessors had begun some years earlier. Monnett also assisted Senator H. E. Valentine in the investigation of trust problems undertaken by a committee of the state senate in 1898. As a result of this inquiry the legislature enacted the Valentine Act which defined and prohibited various trust practices and specified criminal penalties for violations of the law.

Among the more notable achievements of the Bushnell administration were several pieces of social legislation which gave state authorities more power to regulate the employment and hours of work of minors in factories and mines, improved the working conditions of women in factories, and imposed sanitary standards for bakeries. The general assembly also passed bills substituting electrocution for hanging in the execution of the death sentence, regulating the practice of medicine in the state through the establishment of a board of medical registration and qualification, and authorizing the erection of the judiciary annex to the statehouse. Governor Bushnell took a keen interest in the planning and construction of this building, the cornerstone of which was laid in 1899.

Upon relinquishing the governorship in January 1900, Bushnell resumed the direction of his business interests in Springfield. Shortly thereafter he sold his mower company to the International Harvester Company. At the time of his death, which occurred in January 1904, he was engaged in the promotion of an electric interurban railway to connect Springfield and neighboring cities. He was survived by his widow, two daughters, and a son.

The Ohio State University   Robert H. Bremner

GEORGE K. NASH
1900 - 1904

George Kilbon Nash's election as governor of Ohio in November 1899 climaxed thirty years of faithful service to the Republican party. He was born in 1842 on a farm in York Township, Medina County, Ohio. His family was of New England extraction and of strong anti-slavery views. Young Nash studied at Western Reserve Academy and attended Oberlin College for two years. He entered the Union Army as a private in 1864, serving in the same regiment as Mark Hanna. At the end of the war he came to Columbus, read law, and was admitted to the bar in 1867.

His political career began in 1869 with an appointment as chief clerk in the office of the secretary of state. During the 1870's he was twice elected prosecuting attorney of Franklin County, and in the eighties he served two terms as attorney general in the administration of Governor Charles Foster. It was at this time that he won widespread public notice through the successful prosecution of a lawsuit against the Vanderbilt interests to prevent the merger of two competing railroad lines. Before leaving office Foster appointed Nash to the supreme court commission, a body which assisted the court to clear its docket.

Like Foster, Nash belonged to the Sherman-Hanna-McKinley wing of the Republican party rather than to the Foraker faction. He was Hanna's choice for governor in 1895, but lost the nomination to Asa Bushnell, a Foraker man. Two years later, after Hanna had won control of the party machinery, Nash was named chairman of the Republican state executive committee. He supported Hanna's candidacy for election to the United States Senate in 1898 and, with the aid of Hanna and the endorsement of Boss Cox of Cincinnati, received the Republican nomination for governor in 1899. In the campaign of 1899 Nash defeated John R. McLean, the Democratic candidate, and Samuel M. Jones, mayor of Toledo, who ran as an independent. He was reelected in 1901 by a substantial plurality over James Kilbourne, Democrat, of Columbus.

Nash enjoyed a reputation as a strong governor and he gave the state a businessman's administration. He used the prestige and authority of his office to push the measures he favored through the legislature and to block those that he opposed. He supported a constitutional amendment, ratified in 1903, which conferred a limited veto power on the governor; established a uniform auditing system for state offices and institutions; and conducted vigorous investigations of several state schools and hospitals. His administration repeatedly intervened in the affairs of the larger cities of the state.

Many of the laws enacted and executive actions taken during Nash's four years in office can be understood only in the light of the concern aroused in the Hanna wing of the Republican party by the policies and popularity of municipal reformers in three of the major cities in Ohio: the fusion (anti-Cox) group in Cincinnati, "Golden Rule" Jones in Toledo, and Tom L. Johnson in Cleveland. Among the first bills considered by the general assembly in 1900 was one which reorganized the government of Cincinnati in a manner that permitted the Cox machine to return to power. In 1902 the legislature passed an act removing control of the Toledo police force from Mayor Jones and vesting it in a bipartisan board appointed by the governor; a similar measure transferred the supervision of the Cleveland park system from city officials to a county board.

Statutes of this kind were made possible, despite a constitutional prohibition of special legislation, by the long-established legislative practice of classifying municipalities in such a way that there was usually only one city in a given classification. Thus laws could be passed referring to "cities of the first class of the second grade" which were seemingly general in application but actually were directed at one particular city. The municipal classification system had been sanctioned by the state supreme court in a series of decisions extending over many years but, in two cases decided on June 27, 1902, the court reversed its stand. One suit involved the Toledo police law, which was ruled invalid as special legislation. The other case concerned the Cleveland city charter, and restored certain independent powers to that city.

The Cleveland charter case had been instituted by Nash's attorney general, John M. Sheets, apparently in order to bar Mayor Johnson and the city council of Cleveland from taking action prejudicial to Mark Hanna's street railway company. The effect of the two decisions was to upset the government of virtually every city in Ohio, since practically all of them had been chartered by special acts of the legislature. To correct the situation the governor summoned a special session of the general assembly.

In framing the new code both Nash and the legislature ignored the recommendations of a commission appointed in the second Bushnell administration to formulate a uniform system of municipal law. The model code, drawn up by the commission and reported to the legislature in 1900, proposed the federal plan of city government, provided for strong popular control over the granting of franchises, and permitted municipal ownership of public utilities. Nash, however, opposed the centralization of executive power in the office of mayor, favored the administration of police departments by bipartisan boards appointed by and responsible to the governor, and believed it necessary to limit the power of cities to tax, assess, borrow money, and contract debts. In general his views on municipal government were in harmony with those of Boss Cox and Senators Hanna and Foraker, all of whom took an active interest in the preparation of the new code.

As adopted the new municipal code followed the general lines laid down by the governor in his message to the special session of the general assembly. In the opinion of a national magazine the legislation represented "a distinct disappointment to municipal reformers," and even Nash admitted that it was "not perfect." Although the legislature refused to accept the principle of administering local affairs through boards appointed by state officials, the general result of the measure enacted was to weaken the powers of mayors and divide executive responsibility among numerous elective boards, some of them bipartisan in composition. The utility franchise issue was avoided for the time being; the code contained no plan for controlling the issuance of franchises, but referred the problem to a new commission.

Governor Nash's chief interest and major achievement lay in the field of taxation. During his administrations, laws were passed requiring an annual report from corporations and the payment of a fee of one-tenth of one percent upon the capital actually invested in them; the public utility tax was raised from one-half of one percent to one percent of gross receipts; and insurance companies chartered in other states were taxed two and one-half percent of their gross receipts in Ohio. Revenue obtained from the new taxes enabled the Nash administration to effect a reduction in the direct property tax from 28 to 13½ cents per hundred dollars of valuation.

As Nash pointed out, he was no foe of corporations. He supported the amendment repealing the double liability clause in the state constitution. The annual report required of corporations was, in his words, "not inquisitorial," and the tax laws he sponsored were scarcely burdensome to the businesses involved. Under his plan public utility franchises were left untaxed and business firms benefited by the scaling down of the direct levy on general property. Furthermore the Nash administration remitted increases in tax valuations assessed against public utilities by Cleveland officials, and protected railroads against proposed increases in the tax valuations of their properties.

Nash died on October 28, 1904, eight months after leaving office. He had been preceded in death by his wife and only child, a daughter.

The Ohio State University   ROBERT H. BREMNER

MYRON T. HERRICK
1904 - 1906

When, on the morning of May 21, 1927, the word reached Ambassador Myron T. Herrick that Charles A. Lindbergh was nearing France on the first solo flight from America, he sensed both a duty and an opportunity. When the flyer landed at Le Bourget Field, he was met by a tremendous crowd, including Ambassador Herrick, who gave him a hearty welcome and assumed charge of his entertainment and itinerary. The reception and friendship tendered by the ambassador were but an expression of the kindliness and graciousness which had characterized the man.

It was a far cry from this dramatic episode to the circumstances of Herrick's birth at Huntington, Lorain County, Ohio, on October 9, 1854. The boy, who was born in a cabin built by his grandfather, received his first incentive to go to college from Henry Ward Beecher's novel, *Norwood,* in which the hero worked his way through school. At the age of thirteen Myron Herrick rode a horse to Oberlin to see a college commencement for the first time. Before long he was at Oberlin for

140

study, doing odd jobs to defray expenses. As soon as he could qualify, he taught school for two years. Then he left on a business venture to St. Louis, where he wrote articles for a newspaper, and a reporting trip through the Kansas cattle country. Home again with 700 dollars, he spent two years at Ohio Wesleyan University before leaving to study law in Cleveland.

Passing the bar examination in 1878, he started his professional career in Cleveland. His energy and business contacts led him into business, and he participated in the formation of the Cleveland Hardware Company, the National Carbon Company, and the Euclid Avenue National Bank, of which he became a director. At one point he was induced to sign the note of a client, who quickly failed. Although he could have escaped responsibility through a technicality, Herrick, with the support of his young wife, Carolyn Parmely, assumed the debt. This act so impressed certain of the influential bank directors, notably Marcus A. Hanna, that they directed to him sufficient business to pay the entire obligation.

In 1886 the thriving Society for Savings, a Cleveland bank, offered him the post of secretary. In large part it was upon the recommendation of Hanna, who said, "He is young and he may not know anything about banking but I can tell you one thing, he will not steal your money." Apart from his knowledge of banking, Cleveland businessmen valued his honesty, charm, and gracious manners, which overcame many a barrier in the business world. Serving his apprenticeship under the astute Samuel H. Mather, he became successively president and chairman of the board of the Society for Savings, and forwarded the building of its million-dollar home on the Public Square.

It was natural that the young attorney, banker, and businessman should become interested in civic affairs and politics. From 1885 to 1888 he served creditably and courageously on the Cleveland City Council. In the latter year he won the designation of first delegate to the Republican national convention over Mark Hanna, but won the latter's friendship by graciously suggesting that he should receive that honor. He was now a factor to be reckoned with in politics. Subsequently he served on the state executive committee, as Ohio commissioner to the centennial of Washington's inauguration, as presidential elector in 1892, as a member of Governor McKinley's staff, and as a delegate to the Republican national convention in 1896.

Herrick's entry into elective state office came in 1903 at the suggestion of Senator Hanna. He was nominated for governor by acclamation and was opposed by the colorful Tom L. Johnson, who stressed the single-tax theories of Henry George. In the election Herrick received a plurality of 113,812.

After his inauguration on January 11, 1904, Governor Herrick, was confronted with the problems and intricacies of Ohio Republican politics, torn into factions led by Senator Hanna, George B. Cox of Cincinnati, and Senator Joseph B. Foraker. Although he paid careful attention to sound financial practices and efficient administration, he reaped a whirlwind of discontent from certain of his actions. When Herrick approved a school bill opposed by Cuyahoga interests, it was said bitterly that he had "surrendered to Cox." When the Chisholm Bill was passed allowing betting at race tracks, Herrick, who was the first governor of the state to have the veto power, disapproved the bill on constitutional and moral grounds. Many Cleveland friends thought that he was committed otherwise and protested strongly. The church groups who approved his action soon turned against him over the local option issue.

When the Brannock Bill, a local option bill, was nearing passage he forced certain changes which he regarded as necessary to make it a fair and workable measure. The anti-saloon leaders considered the action a defeat for themselves, and succeeded in alienating the church support which Herrick had gained through the veto of the race track bill. At the same time the liquor interests resented any legislation on the subject. All this came to a focus in the next election, in the fall of 1905, when Governor Herrick lost to the Democratic nominee, John M. Pattison, and returned to his business interests in Cleveland.

To his three distinct careers—law, politics, and business—Herrick was soon to add a fourth and more distinguished career in the diplomatic service. Both McKinley and Roosevelt had offered Herrick the ambassadorship to Italy. In both instances he preferred to remain in business, but in 1912, when President Taft offered him the diplomatic post at Paris, he accepted, with the understanding that he would prepare a report on rural credit systems in Europe, a purpose which he carried out. Upon the inauguration of Woodrow Wilson, Ambassador Herrick offered his resignation. He carried on, however, at the president's request, and it was not until November 28, 1914, that he was relieved.

It was during this period that he performed his most distinguished service. With the outbreak of the war, he was asked to care for the interests of the Central Powers in addition to fulfilling the greatly augmented duties to his own country. A decision of great importance was that to stay at his post as the Germans approached in what appeared to be an overpowering thrust toward Paris. The French government left for Bordeaux on September 2, 1914, and nearly all the diplomatic corps followed immediately. Herrick decided to remain to represent his country's interests in the event of a German occupation of the city. His burdens were increased by the necessity of representing various countries whose representatives had gone to Bordeaux. During this period he narrowly escaped a German bomb—an incident widely commented upon as indicating his devotion to duty. The Germans were thrown back, the city was saved, and Herrick, because of his devotion to duty, was enshrined in the hearts of the French people.

The year 1921 saw him again in Paris as ambassador. He was greeted by the French as an old and true friend. With his customary graciousness he labored for eight years in the difficult post-war reconstruction period. The hard work was lightened by his pleasant relationships, but his strength gradually failed. Weakened by his exertions in attending Marshall Foch's funeral, he died quietly on Easter Sunday, March 31, 1929. As a token of appreciation the French government sent the cruiser *Tourville* to take his remains back to his native land.

Ambassador Herrick was survived by his son, Parmely Webb Herrick. Mrs. Herrick had died in 1918.

Pensacola Junior College, Pensacola, Florida   RUSSELL H. ANDERSON

JOHN M. PATTISON
1906

The record of Ohio's forty-third governor, John M. Pattison, is that of a man eminently successful in business and capable of winning his way in politics by sheer force of character. Governor Pattison was born near Owensville, Clermont County, Ohio, on June 13, 1847, the son of Mary Duckwall and William Pattison, a country merchant. As a youth, John worked in his father's store and on neighboring farms.

In 1864, before he was seventeen years old, he joined the 153d Ohio Volunteer Infantry. Upon his return home from the war, he entered Ohio Wesleyan University at Delaware. To support himself while attending the university, he taught school in winter and worked in the harvest fields in summer. Though he spent not more than twenty months on the campus, he graduated with his class in 1869.

After graduation, Pattison took charge of an agency for the Union Central Life Insurance Company in Bloomington, Illinois. Tiring of the insurance business, he returned to Cincinnati to study law in the office of Alfred Yaple. He was admitted to the bar in 1872. He became the attorney for the Cincinnati and Marietta Railroad, but resigned when he was elected to the state legislature from Hamilton County in 1873. He declined renomination because he wished to devote his time to his profession. Pattison became a member of the firm of Yaple, Moos, and Pattison and practiced law with that firm for ten years. During three of those ten years he edited a law magazine. From 1874 to 1876 he was attorney for the Committee of Safety, a nonpartisan organization in Cincinnati for the promotion of civic welfare.

On December 10, 1879, Pattison was married to Aletheia Williams, the daughter of William G. Williams, professor of Greek at Ohio Wesleyan University. They became the parents of two daughters and one son—Aletheia, Ernestine, and John. After the death of his wife, Pattison married her sister, Anna Williams.

In 1881 Pattison was elected vice president and manager of the Union Central Life Insurance Company. Under his management the company enjoyed a remarkable expansion. He became its president in 1891.

Pattison reentered politics in 1890, when, against his wishes, he was nominated to fill a vacany in the state senate for the Clermont-Brown counties district. The redistribution of the congressional districts was about to be made, and since that would determine the political complexion of Ohio's representation in congress, the campaign attracted national attention. Pattison won the election with the largest vote on record in Clermont County for a state office. In 1891 he was elected to congress, where he helped to secure one of the first appropriations for the rural free delivery of mail. Pattison was renominated but defeated, because his district had been made so strongly Republican by the recent Republican gerrymander that it was impossible for a Democrat to be elected. At the expiration of his term in 1893, he returned to the Union Central Life Insurance Company in Cincinnati.

By 1905 fourteen years of Republican rule had created a desire among the people for a change. Governor Myron T. Herrick had antagonized the Anti-Saloon League and other interests, and there was a charge of graft in the statehouse. The Republican state convention placed the party squarely against the temperance movement and against all disloyalty to Governor Herrick. In the convention William Howard Taft spoke out against bossism, and voters remembered that George B.

Cox, notorious Republican boss of Hamilton County, had helped to elect Governor Herrick.

Encouraged by Republican blunders, the Ohio Democrats were full of hope when they met in convention in June 1905. Pattison was firmly supported by the Democrats in the rural communities, while he was strongly opposed by the urban Democrats. He opposed a contest over the chairmanship of the convention, but that body ignored the chairman chosen by the committee and made Michael Daugherty permanent chairman. Daugherty's scathing attack upon Mark Hanna and his bitter arraignment of the Republican party constituted what the Democrats considered a great political philippic. The most important planks of the platform were a denunciation of boss rule and a plea for municipal ownership of public utilities. Pattison gained the nomination, and with this irreproachable candidate, the Democrats entered the campaign undaunted by the large plurality of the Republican party in the national election of 1904.

Pattison was a strict observer of the Sabbath and an ardent temperance man. He had advocated the Sunday closing law and had made a speech in congress opposing the opening of the World's Fair in Chicago on the Sabbath Day. Pattison was not an uncompromising partisan; he was a man of high intelligence and outstanding executive ability; his character was unimpeachable. He was elected governor with a plurality of more than 43,000 votes, though the Democratic candidates for all the other state offices were soundly defeated. Pattison's victory was clearly a personal achievement.

On January 8, 1906, he read his inaugural address in a firm clear voice, but he looked frail and worn. The strain of the campaign had sapped his strength. He returned to his office for a little while and left it never to return.

Governor Pattison lived through only one session of the general assembly. In April he left the executive mansion for Christ Hospital in Cincinnati. He was later removed to his home in Milford, Clermont County, and died there on June 18.

The most notable legislation passed during his short administration concerned liquor, county salaries and funds, and railroads. The saloon tax was raised from 350 to 1,000 dollars, and a law was passed which authorized local option on the sale of liquor in residential districts. Idle county funds were put to work as loans, the accrued interest to be paid into county treasuries; salaries were provided for county officials; and fees were abolished. A two-cent railroad fare was established, and the office of commissioner of railroads and telegraphs was superseded by a railroad commission of three members. The regulation of railroads was a live issue in congress and in many state legislatures at that time.

Oxford, Ohio   OPHIA D. SMITH

ANDREW L. HARRIS
1906 - 1909

Ohio's forty-fourth governor, Andrew L. Harris, the last of the Civil War veteran governors of Ohio, acceded to that position on the death of John M. Pattison, June 18, 1906.

The "farmer statesman" was born November 17, 1835, on a farm in Butler County, Ohio. His parents, Benjamin and Nancy Lintner Harris, were of Irish and German ancestry and both were natives of Ohio. Primarily a farmer, his father had also been a school teacher and had served in minor township offices. In 1838 the Harris family moved to a farm in Preble County, where young Harris grew to manhood. Through the winter seasons he attended country public schools, and in 1857 he entered Miami University.

After graduating from college in 1860, Harris returned to help on his father's farm and to read law in the firm of Thompson and Harris in Eaton, the county seat. When the call was issued by President Lincoln in April 1861, Harris enlisted as a private. He saw active service in eighteen battles, some of which were major engagements of the

Civil War. At the battle of McDowell in Virginia he was seriously wounded and his right arm permanently disabled by gun shot. He was also wounded in the fighting at Gettysburg. Harris received a number of promotions and when his regimental commander was killed in action at Chancellorsville, he was made colonel and commander. On January 15, 1865, he was mustered out. Further recognition was given on March 13, 1866, when he was breveted bridgadier general for "gallant and meritorious" service during the war.

Wounds kept him from manual labor on the farm in Preble County, so Harris continued preparing for the bar. In April 1865 he was admitted and began to practice in Eaton. A few months later, in October 1865, he was married to Caroline Conger, a Preble County farmer's daughter by whom he had one son. The people of Preble and Montgomery counties elected Harris as a Republican to represent them in the senate of the fifty-seventh general assembly of 1866-67. With Robert Miller of Eaton a law partnership was formed in 1866 that was to continue for ten years. In 1875 and again in 1878 Harris was elected probate judge of Preble County. After that term, hoping to retire from public life, he returned to the farm.

This dream was to be short-lived, however, because a succession of public offices was soon to follow. In 1885 and 1887 he was elected to serve in the house of representatives of the sixty-seventh and sixty-eighth general assemblies. Governor Foraker appointed him, in 1889, a trustee of the Ohio Soldiers' and Sailors' Orphans' Home. In both the elections of 1891 and 1893 he was made lieutenant governor and served under William McKinley. Later, when McKinley was president, he appointed Harris to the federal industrial commission on trusts and industrial combinations and made him chairman of the subcommission on agriculture and agricultural labor. He served in this capacity from 1898 to 1902. Once more he retired to private life and his Preble County farm.

In the state elections of 1905, when political exigencies demanded a soldier as a running mate to Governor Herrick, Harris was again nominated as lieutenant governor. Although Herrick was defeated, Harris and the rest of the Republican slate were elected by substantial majorities. On June 18, 1906, Governor Pattison died, and Harris then became the chief executive. Because of a constitutional amendment adopted in 1905 providing that subsequent elections be held in even numbered years, the Pattison-Harris administration was to run for three years, 1906-9. All but about five months of this term was left to Harris.

Under Governor Harris considerable progressive legislation was enacted. A pure food and drug law was passed; conservation measures were adopted; a bureau of vital statistics was established; corporations were forbidden to contribute or to use money for political purposes; and a measure for the regulation and inspection of building and loan savings associations was passed. The Republican state convention in 1908 nominated Harris for governor by acclamation, but in the election he and the Republican candidate for treasurer lost to the Democrats. He had incurred the enmity of the liquor interests by the passage of a local option law, the Rose Law, which had enabled well over half of the counties of the state to go dry. He had long championed temperance measures as a state legislator and as governor, but his position on the question was well in advance of public sentiment at this time.

Because of the constitutional amendment changing election dates there was to be no scheduled meeting of the general assembly in 1909. In this contingency Harris called the seventy-eighth general assembly to meet in extraordinary session in January 1909. Election of a United States Senator, appropriations, and other routine measures were to be considered. Harris recommended the establishment of a department of auditing and inspection and the employment of the competitive bidding principle to be applied by all state officers in purchasing supplies, but "no enactments of any note resulted."

Harris went back to the farm once more where he spent the remainder of his days. The "farmer statesman" died of heart trouble in Eaton on September 13, 1915. Although public service took him to high places, he was ever aware of his attachment to the common people. He represented and was responsive to the typical attitude of the rural Ohio of that day.

Miami University   DWIGHT L. SMITH

JUDSON HARMON
1909 - 1913

In the presidential year of 1908 the voters of Ohio chose the Republican favorite son, William Howard Taft, for the presidency and a Democrat, Judson Harmon, for the governorship. This anomalous result reflected a popular reaction against a long period of Republican misrule of the state government and a public confidence in the Democratic standard bearer that he would introduce clean, efficient government in Ohio.

Harmon, an elder statesman of the party just turned sixty-two, inspired such trust. His presence was commanding, disclosing a character strong yet benevolent. He was big framed, erect of bearing, with a ruddy complexion and a sandy, cropped mustache. His eyes, set under shaggy brows, had a piercing look, yet frequently were lit with flashes of kindness; his firm mouth broke easily into a smile or hearty laugh. His speech was plain, blunt, easily assimilable. He had a reputation for exemplary probity.

He was born on February 3, 1846, at Newtown in Hamilton County,

Ohio, the son of a Baptist minister, and worked his way through Denison University and the Cincinnati Law School. He married Olivia Scobey of Hamilton in 1870.

Settling in Cincinnati in 1869 to practice his profession, he became a prominent attorney and won a reputation as a judge in both the common pleas and superior courts. Although he had been inclined toward the Republican party in the Civil War period, he revolted against the harsh Reconstruction program and eventually became firmly affiliated with the Democratic party. President Cleveland in 1895 appointed him to the attorney generalship where he won renown by preparing and prosecuting two important antitrust suits.

Although politically inactive after retirement from his cabinet post in 1897, he did not disappear from the public eye. He was remarkably successful as a receiver in reorganizing three railroads and nursing them back to financial health. In 1905 he briefly shot into national prominence as a result of his investigations of alleged violations by the Santa Fe Railroad of the law prohibiting rebates. His findings implicated the company officers, and he insisted that they should be indicted. President Theodore Roosevelt refused, ruling that only the corporation should be held responsible for criminal acts. In a public letter Harmon defended his position: "The evils with which we are now confronted are corporate in name but individual in fact. Guilt is always personal."

This principle which applied equally well to officers of government was central to his thinking. Like his chieftain, Grover Cleveland, he also believed that public office is a public trust. Economy and business efficiency in the management of public affairs, fairness towards all, favoritism towards none, and limited exercise of governmental power —these were the political convictions to which he steadfastly adhered. Essentially conservative, he seemed troubled and perplexed by the new political trend, espoused by the Tom Johnson radical Democrats, toward direct democracy, economic equality, and humanitarian reform. Progressives commended him for his old-fashioned virtues, but they never accepted him as one of them.

Harmon served as governor for two terms, winning reelection in 1910 by a 100,000 plurality over his Republican rival, Warren G. Harding. During these four years he put in order the state administration, exposing a major scandal in the corrupt handling of state funds, eliminating peculation and waste in a half dozen departments, replacing the incompetent with competent men, and elevating the tone of government. He counted as his greatest legislative achievements four measures. Three of them increased economy and efficiency: changes in the depository laws, making mandatory a proper accounting of the people's money; the centralization of the management of the state's penal and charitable institutions; and a one percent tax limit law. Only the fourth was a humanitarian measure, Ohio's first employers' liability law.

This selection is as instructive for what it omits as for what it includes in revealing Harmon's conservative temper and outlook. Progressives considered of equal, if not greater, importance other major items adopted: the creation of Ohio's first public service commission and a tax commission, both with real powers to correct existing discriminations; ratification of the federal income tax amendment; a maximum-hour law for working women; the Oregon plan for electing United States senators; and the initiative and referendum for cities. Although to some of these enactments Harmon was openly sympathetic, to others he was indifferent, even hostile.

By 1912 his political aspirations had soared beyond the governorship to the presidency itself. His record made him a highly "available" candidate. Although he was the choice of Democratic conservatives, many party progressives felt his usefulness had passed and were searching for a point of attack. Harmon made one for them, when on February 8, 1912, he delivered his fateful address to the Ohio Constitutional Convention opposing the initiative and referendum and other popular reforms. Admirable as it was to place personal conviction above political expediency, he nevertheless revealed that he was out of tune with the progressive thinking of the day. From that hour his chances for the presidential nomination and continued leadership of the Ohio Democracy were doomed.

The story of the 1912 convention is well known. No Harmon boom developed, partly because he entered the convention with a divided Ohio delegation. The nomination of Wilson and the ascendancy of the progressive wing struck the Ohioan's political death knell. In January 1913 Harmon returned to Cincinnati, where he resumed his law practice and taught for many years in the Cincinnati Law School. Efforts to entice him back into politics were unavailing. He died in Cincinnati on February 22, 1927, survived by three daughters.

Harmon merits a place among Ohio's outstanding governors. He introduced a tough moral fiber into a government grown flabby; he was fearless in pursuing what he believed to be right policy, offending the spoilsmen of the party when he refused to fire competent Republicans, alarming the Democratic stalwarts by insisting upon the impartial prosecution of corrupt officials regardless of party label. Although his own political thinking harked back to an earlier era, he was flexible enough to accept some of the conclusions of the progressives without agreeing with their premises. In reinvigorating the state administration, he prepared the ground for the ultimate triumph of progressive ideas. He restored to the people a confidence that government could be trusted to play the more vigorous role demanded by the radical humanitarian reformers.

Kenyon College   LANDON WARNER

JAMES M. COX
1913 - 1915, 1917 - 1921

On a bright, crisp January day in 1913 crowds gathered in Columbus to attend the inauguration of the governor-elect, James M. Cox. They lined the approach to the capitol, beating time to the rhythms of the bands, waving flags and streamers, and shouting, "Hello, Jimmy," to the trim, youthful figure, who was about to take the oath of office. Moved by this spontaneous display of enthusiasm, the new governor voiced with brevity and earnest simplicity his own deep emotion: "We are entering upon a new day. . . . The forces of human intelligence have carried us to a point of higher moral vision, and it would have been a distinct anomaly of history if government had not been carried on in the progress of the time. . . . I sense therefore the sublime responsibility of this hour!"

The progressive movement had reached its crest in Ohio. In the three-cornered contest of 1912 Cox had won not only because the new Progressive party had split the Republican ranks but, even more important, because he was more genuinely committed to the cause of reform than either of his opponents. He had run on a platform which embodied every major progressive plank; he had campaigned strenuously for the constitutional amendments submitted to the Ohio voters in September 1912; he entered office dedicated to redeeming the constitutional mandate and promoting Ohio to the vanguard of progressive states.

Few men were better equipped by experience, temperament, and ability to perform this task. Reared on his father's farm near Dayton, where he was born on March 31, 1870, he became successively school teacher, printer's devil, newspaper reporter, and secretary to Congressman Paul Sorg. In 1898 he entered upon his lifetime work as the editor-publisher of the *Dayton Daily News,* adding in 1905 another Ohio paper, the *Springfield News.* His active political career began in 1908, when he was elected to congress for the first of two terms.

Although born into the Democratic fold he did not take his party allegiance for granted. As a young man he identified himself with the militant wing—dissenters in the conservative Republican environment of Ohio. In his autobiography, *Journey Through My Years,* he documents his receptiveness to new ideas and new forces: the radical philosophy of the Populists; the jabs of the muckrakers at the old order; the spirit of regeneration introduced by Sam Jones and Tom Johnson in their respective cities of Toledo and Cleveland; and the house of representatives "revolution" of 1909-11, in which he was one of the rebels. The only bar across his record from the progressive viewpoint was his close association with a reactionary Democratic boss in Dayton —a friendship dictated by political necessity, not by ideological compatability.

By the time Cox was installed in the governor's office he had dispelled the doubts about the genuineness of his progressivism. His first message to the legislature mapped out a fifty-six point program embracing every reform for which there was a popular demand. Conscious of his responsibility for the enactment of these proposals, he boldly assumed leadership of legislative tactics and strategy, brilliantly improvising techniques to assure the success of his campaign.

In preparing the agenda he assigned the work of bill-drafting to experts and called upon Wisconsin reformers, leading penologists, and others for aid. He exercised a strong hand in the organization of the assembly and sought to hold the members in line by persuading that body to adopt an act regulating lobbyists and by witholding the distribution of patronage until the end of the session. A legislative reference bureau was established at the outset to aid in efficient bill-drafting, and the governor kept a personal file on the progress of each proposal in the legislature. Cox's enemies accused him of molding the assembly "until it became as plastic as clay in the master potter's hands." Actually there were remarkably few "clay" figures in the statehouse. The members, many possessed of surpassing ability and integrity, were not servants of but co-workers with the governor, sharing together a community of interest.

At the end of a ninety-day session almost the entire program had been written into statute—proof enough of Cox's extraordinary drive and skill. Tag ends were completed in two short special sessions in 1914. Only the major items can be mentioned in this brief survey. The long sought reforms for more direct democracy were completed by the adoption of a direct primary law and safeguards for the use of the initiative and referendum. The courts were reorganized and judicial procedure was altered. Vast changes were made in the state administration through the extension of the civil service law, authorization of a budget commissioner, centralization of the tax machinery, and the creation of commissions based on the Wisconsin model to insure unified management of industrial and agricultural policies. Basic conservation legislation and a good-roads program were initiated. An optional municipal charter law was approved for cities which had won the right to home rule by constitutional amendment. The rural school code was rewritten. The most outstanding legacy from this session was the humanitarian legislation: the model workmen's compensation act, mothers' pension law, children's code, bureau of juvenile research act, and laws which produced enlightened changes in the penal system which placed Ohio in the front ranks in prison reform.

Cox was easily renominated in 1914 and ran on his record of "promises fulfilled," proposing, if reelected, "an era of legislative rest." Although contingent reasons contributed, the citizens of Ohio had apparently grown tired of reformers and cast a small plurality for the Republican Frank B. Willis. Two years later Cox again sought a personal vindication of his program, little of which had been altered during two years of Republican rule. By a record-thin margin he defeated

Willis, and in 1918 repeated his victory over the same rival and became the first Ohio governor to serve three full terms.

During his last two administrations reform laws were refined in the light of experience but no new ones were added. Our entry into World War I three months after his second inauguration precipitated a new set of problems. The governor had to step into labor disputes which threatened a production stoppage. His uncommon common sense and his trust in labor's good will succeeded in holding industrial strife to a minimum. He was responsible for keeping at a high pitch civilian response to the war effort. As part of the program to strengthen morale he backed the controversial law barring the teaching of German in Ohio schools, which the United States Supreme Court later held unconstitutional.

Catapulted into national prominence by his thrice-repeated victories in Ohio, he was nominated for president by his party in 1920 and campaigned in favor of Wilson's program for America's entry into the League of Nations. After Cox's defeat he retired from active politics, occasionally entering party counsels as an elder statesman. In 1933 he was a member of the American delegation to the ill-starred World Monetary and Economic Conference in London. He has added to his newspaper holdings by the purchase of papers in Atlanta, Georgia, and Miami, Florida. Now in his eighty-fifth year, he divides his time between Dayton and Miami, keeping a watchful eye over his journalistic enterprises.

Cox's first administration is considered by many competent judges as the most distinguished in Ohio's recent history. Though many helped, the governor made the greatest single contribution. It was his shrewd political sense, his administrative talent, and his deep humanitarian instinct which made possible the progressive triumph. If he lost his zeal for reform by 1916, so had the Ohio public and many of his party colleagues. As the chief executive during the war years he made good his aim of giving Ohio a war record of which it would be proud.

Governor Cox was married twice and was the father of six children, one of whom died in infancy.

Kenyon College   LANDON WARNER

FRANK B. WILLIS
1915 - 1917

In the early spring of 1928 Senator Frank B. Willis declared that the approaching struggle in the Ohio primary election would not be a "powder-puff or pink tea" affair. At the time the senior senator from the Buckeye state was starting a vigorous campaign for the Republican presidential nomination. He entered the fray with an obvious enthusiasm, born of a deep love of politics and political battles. It had been thirty-two years since the crucial campaign of 1896, when he first worked for the Republican party, and Willis indicated he was going to utilize his long experience in the important presidential contest.

A survey of his political background reveals service in the state of Ohio as legislator and governor, in addition to federal service in the house of representatives and the senate. In short it was a crowded career, stretching back to his birth in 1871 in Delaware County, Ohio. The Willis family lived on a farm and had a considerable interest in the wool trade. The young boy attended a small country school where he was encouraged to go on for further academic work. As a result he taught school, chopped wood, and did odd jobs to finance his way through Ohio Northern University. Graduating in 1893, he remained with the university on its teaching staff. Although he was popular with the students, political interests soon cut into his teaching activities.

Following the 1896 election, Willis conducted a successful house to house campaign for a seat in the state legislature three years later. As a young Republican serving a traditionally Democratic district he soon created much favorable comment concerning his political future. One veteran statehouse observer wrote, "Although but 31 years of age he is already well-known throughout the state, and during the recent session of the . . . General Assembly, the attention of the commonwealth and the country as well, was drawn to a tax bill bearing his name." The Willis law provided for a tax on corporations chartered by the state and foreign corporations operating in the state. It required the payment of sums equal to a fixed percentage of the capital stock of the various corporations.

In 1904 the young lawmaker tried to secure the Republican nomination for a congressional seat, but his efforts were defeated and he returned to Ohio Northern. During this entire period, Willis had been studying law. He took the bar examination in 1906 and passed with the highest score. For the next four years his teaching was centered primarily in the field of law. College work could not hold Willis, however, and he reentered politics in 1910. After obtaining the party's blessing, he defeated his Democratic opponent in a struggle for the eighth congressional seat. In 1912 he was one of three Ohio Republican congressmen returned to their posts. Three years in Washington, where he proved himself in house debates, opened the way to the governorship.

Willis was nominated for the gubernatorial race under the terms of the new direct primary law. The first Republican so selected, he demonstrated his popularity with the party organization and the voters. Willis was a clever and challenging campaigner. A handsome man of imposing stature, he was at his best at informal party rallies, church socials, and rural get-togethers. He had a rich, booming voice which could be fashioned to meet any demand. Perhaps his greatest political asset was his uncanny ability to remember faces and names.

The progressive spirit which engulfed the American people during the early years of the twentieth century influenced the official Republican declarations during the 1914 campaign. The party favored increased compensation for injured workmen, and endorsed "the eight-hour system of daily labor wherever practicable." It also went on record as recognizing "the wider claims of the people upon their goverment for legislation to promote social justice," and pledged full cooperation "in the broader movement for human welfare." The campaign itself was a three-man race with the spotlight focused upon Governor James Cox and Willis. The Progressive candidate pursued a hopeless cause; Willis emerged the victor with a plurality of the votes cast.

In his inaugural address Governor Willis spoke at some length on the challenge of executive centralization to the proper functioning of free government. He concluded his plea for respect of the traditional "division of governmental functions" with the hopeful assertion, "It were folly to say this system is the acme of perfection, yet it is only the plain truth to state that according to the judgement of the intelligence of the world it is the best system yet devised by man."

The Willis administration, as it sought to protect the free system of government, stressed "economy and retrenchment." The governor provided a strong influence against needless and excessive legislative activity. Among the important measures approved by Willis were those revising the road laws of the state, reorganizing the state militia, reorganizing the civil service commission, providing elected rather than appointed local assessment officers, revamping the entire liquor licensing system, and regulating the appointment of county agricultural agents. Executive action was of necessity sharp and direct upon occasion. In January 1916 Willis ordered part of the militia to East Youngstown to quell violence that had broken out during a steel strike. When the Mexican border troubles took a turn for the worse, he mobilized the entire Ohio National Guard.

The 1916 gubernatorial contest was a comparatively quiet affair, overshadowed by the presidential race. Willis lost to former Governor Cox as both men stressed economy and tax reform. A third attempt to gain the governor's chair in 1918 likewise resulted in a defeat for Willis, with prohibition playing an important role in the decision. At this low point in his career he found an opening for a higher honor. Competing for Warren G. Harding's senate post, Willis overwhelmed his opponent, W. A. Julian, in 1920.

Frank Willis vaulted into national prominence with his smashing victory and his important role in the Harding campaign. As a senator he favored a high tariff and veterans' aid and opposed the League of Nations and any program of internationalism. After eight years in the senate his name was put forward for the presidency. He was a sincere, loyal Republican, linked with the conservative wing of the party. A powerful orator, he knew how to grasp the feelings of his audience and turn them to his advantage. Yet for all of his experience he had not gained the actual leadership of the party—a fact he recognized himself. His fighting campaign of 1928 never reached the point of decision, for Willis died dramatically in the midst of a political rally seeking to advance his leadership.

Senator Willis was survived by his wife and daughter Helen, both of whom are living in Delaware, Ohio.

Ohio Wesleyan University   RICHARD W. SMITH

HARRY L. DAVIS
1921 - 1923

Harry L. Davis liked being mayor of Cleveland so well that he returned to that office after serving Ohio as its forty-ninth governor. He previously had served three terms as mayor of the state's great metropolis.

Davis rode into the governor's office on the Republican landslide in 1920 which also sent Ohio's United States Senator Warren G. Harding to the White House. By this victory Davis administered the only political defeat experienced by A. Victor Donahey in his long career as state auditor, governor, and United States Senator.

At the close of his gubernatorial term, January 10, 1921, to January 8, 1923, Davis did not seek reelection. He returned to his insurance business in Cleveland, but kept a weather eye on politics there and in the state at large. He sought the governorship again in 1924, but this time Donahey, who was completing his first term as the state's chief executive, turned the tables on him. Davis stayed in Cleveland where in due time he sensed growing opposition to the city-manager form of government which the city had adopted. He spearheaded this

163

opposition in a successful political battle which tossed out the city-manager system and restored the offices of mayor and city councilmen. In a couple of years he was back in the mayor's office, 1933-35.

Though the 1920 Republican landslide had provided a top-heavy Republican legislature—only thirteen Democrats in a total membership of 169—Governor Davis found the sailing somewhat rough at times. There were rumblings in the senate for an investigation of some administration activities, and the senate and house soon were at logger-heads over tax legislation and the time of adjournment. The impasse reached the point where the governor, exercising a constitutional preroga-tive seldom before used, prorogued the assembly on May 28, 1921. There were charges that the governor had used this drastic method to send the lawmakers home to forestall a senate investigation of certain state contracts.

Perhaps the most unusual and drastic piece of legislation ever enacted by an Ohio legislature was recommended by Governor Davis to cope with economic conditions brought about by a work stoppage of Ohio coal miners. In a special two-day legislative session called by the governor on September 11, 1922, an emergency law was passed setting up a fuel administrator with powers to fix the price of coal at the mines and at retail outlets and to seize and operate the mines if necessary to obtain sufficient fuel for the state's needs. The fuel adminis-trator functioned until December 1, 1922, when the office was abolished by executive order. In the meantime the mines had resumed operation and the coal shortage had dissipated.

A major piece of legislation sponsored by the governor and one which caused much political furor was the state government reorganiza-tion code whereby scores of state offices and departments were combined under directors responsible to the governor. After a bitter legislative battle during which opponents dubbed it the "Davis Ripper Bill," it was passed as an emergency measure, thus preventing a referendum on it. A supreme court battle in which the emergency feature was attacked resulted in a decision that the legislature was the sole judge as to the emergency character of laws and its decision may not be questioned by the courts. That decision has prevented many new laws from being subjected to a referendum of the voters.

Expansion of Ohio State University's physical plant to its present facilities was started by Governor Davis. In his inaugural address he said: "In Ohio State University the commonwealth has an educational institution which should become the largest and best state institution in the United States. This is evidenced by the development of the institution in recent years, and I desire specifically to ask the co-operation of the General Assembly in the effort which I propose to make to help Ohio State University to attain that goal in the not too distant future." On his recommendation the legislature passed a tax levy of one-eighth of a mill for two years to provide a state university building fund. It was divided seventy-two percent to Ohio State University and fourteen percent each to Miami and Ohio universities. A two-year levy of one-fourth mill for a welfare institution building fund also was provided.

State conservation took on a new meaning under the Davis administration. The first state game preserve, the 15,000-acre Roosevelt Game Preserve in Scioto County, was established.

Other important legislation during the Davis regime included acts establishing a prohibition department to enforce the prohibition of the sale of intoxicants, forbidding political subdivisions to incur debts for current operations, and setting a debt limitation on the subdivisions.

One piece of legislation of which Governor Davis was justly proud was that starting the state on a program of aid for special education and the rehabilitation of crippled children.

Governor Davis' public school education had ended at thirteen years of age when he took his place beside his Welsh immigrant father in the Cleveland steel mills. There he toiled until he was nineteen years old, meanwhile attending night school and business college.

Politics appealed to him while he was yet in his early teens, and he soon was active in the Republican party ranks. When his father was elected to the state legislature, young Davis was appointed a page to run errands for his father and other members of the house. He was elected treasurer of Cleveland in 1909 and six years later was elected mayor of the city. His third successive term as mayor was his stepping stone to the governorship.

Governor Davis was born in Cleveland on January 25, 1878. He died on May 21, 1950. He was married to Lucy V. Fegan of Cleveland on July 16, 1902. They had a son, Harry L., Jr.

Office of the Attorney General of Ohio　　　　　H. H. DAUGHERTY

A. VICTOR DONAHEY
1923 - 1929

Vic Donahey, the first governor of Ohio to serve three consecutive terms, was known as the foremost vote getter of his day. A candidate for elective office eleven times, he was defeated only once, in a landslide of the opposition party. Elected governor as a Democrat, he dealt with Republican general assemblies throughout his tenure. His majority in the election for the United States Senate set a record which has not been broken to the date of this publication.

Alvin Victor Donahey began his political career as A. Victor, then shortened his official signature to A. V., but by the time he ran for governor his name went on the ballot as Vic, as he had come to be known by the people throughout the state. He was born July 7, 1873, on a farm between Cadwallader and West Chester, Tuscarawas County, Ohio, to which Donaheys of Scotch-Irish lineage migrated from Pennsylvania in the first year of Ohio's statehood. His father, John C. Donahey, was a school teacher, farmer, and livestock buyer until elected county clerk in the late 1880's, whereupon he moved with his wife (Catherine

166

Chaney) and three sons to New Philadelphia, the county seat. Of the sons, Vic was the eldest, followed by Hal of later *Cleveland Plain Dealer* cartoonist fame, and Will of Chicago, also a well-known cartoonist and artist.

After elementary schooling at West Chester, Vic Donahey attended high school in New Philadelphia, but quit in his junior year to learn the printing trade, which he pursued for some years in newspaper and job printing plants. He bought a print shop of his own at the age of twenty. He remained a member of the International Typographical Union all through his subsequent public career.

Donahey was married on January 5, 1897, to Mary Edith Harvey of Canal Dover (now Dover). They had twelve children, of whom ten are now living. Soon after his marriage Donahey began his public services by being elected clerk of the Goshen Township board of trustees. In 1905 he was elected county auditor, in which office he served two terms. He was also a member of the board of education. In 1911 he was elected a delegate to the Fourth Ohio Constitutional Convention which met the following year. By political convention time in 1912 he had attracted the attention of party leaders who caused him to be nominated for state auditor. In this office, in which he served two four-year terms, his name became a household word throughout the state by reason of his diligence in the examination and inspection of the accounts and expenditures of public offices—state, district, and local.

The most highly publicized instance, though essentially a minor incident, in the pruning of expense accounts, took place when Auditor Donahey refused to reimburse a judge of the court of appeals the full price of a baked potato, listed on the judge's expense receipt at thirty cents. When the auditor cut this to ten cents, the judge promptly filed in the Supreme Court of Ohio a mandamus suit to compel reimbursement in full. After a flare of publicity the incident became a topic of state-wide gossip and discussion favorable to the auditor, whereupon the judge withdrew his suit.

Nominated without opposition for governor at the 1920 primary election, Donahey suffered in November his only defeat at the polls. In 1922 he was elected governor by a majority of 18,648, in 1924 by 176,842, and in 1926 by 16,766. His majority in 1924 was the largest in the history of the state up to that time.

Known in the common parlance of voters as "Honest Vic" or

the "Watchdog of the Treasury" while state auditor, he became known as "Veto Vic" during the legislative session of his first term, when he vetoed seventy-six bills and appropriations for $4,000,000. In his second term he vetoed forty-five bills and appropriations for $2,000,000; in his third, thirty bills and appropriations for $4,000,000. He vetoed every bill which sought to increase taxes, including that for gasoline taxes which was supported primarily by the farm organizations. When this was passed over his veto, he directed the department of highways to spend nearly all of the proceds on grading and graveling unimproved roads in order to "lift the farmers out of the mud," thus adding 6,900 miles of passably improved roads to the state-financed system.

Outstanding among other vetoes were the Ku Klux Klan bill to require daily Bible reading in the public schools and the Anti-Saloon League's bill to require prohibition law offenders to serve out unpaid fines by manual labor on roads and other public works. On the premise that prohibition enforcement was directed unduly against the poor, he pardoned more than two thousand offenders from jails and work-houses.

Donahey ran for a third term for governor on the pretext that the Republican senate had refused to confirm his appointments to the various quasi-judicial commissions of the state. All his appointments in his third term were senate-approved.

Retiring from the governorship in 1929, Donahey organized the Motorists' Mutual Insurance Company of Columbus, of which he became president. He was named a director of the Ohio National Bank of Columbus. He resided at a home which he had built on an island at Indian Lake, where he spent his leisure in various forms of recreation, fishing, whittling, making artifacts, cooking favorite recipes (including personally smoked hams and other meats) for invited friends, until 1934, when he received a flood of thousands of letters urging him to run for the United States Senate. He was elected by a 437,138 majority. In the senate he was chairman of a joint congressional committee to investigate the TVA, which resulted in a reorganization of the authority. When World War II broke out, he opposed President Roosevelt's proposal for modification of the Neutrality Act, saying the action would mean "cash and carry in 1939, cash and credit in 1940, cash and boys in 1941."

Refusing to run for reelection, he returned to his insurance business in 1941. After several years of failing health he died of histoplasmosis capsulatum, a rare malignancy of the blood, on April 8, 1946. He is buried in Schoenbrunn Cemetery, New Philadelphia.

Ohio State Journal   J. A. Meckstroth

MYERS Y. COOPER
1929 - 1931

Myers Y. Cooper, Cincinnati businessman and prominent Republican leader, was inaugurated as the fifty-first governor of Ohio on January 14, 1929. Born on a hill farm in Licking County, Ohio, on November 25, 1873, he was the youngest of eleven children of Lemuel and Ann Cooper, who had come to Ohio from Pennsylvania soon after the Civil War. He was educated in the one-room country school at Echo and at the National Normal University at Lebanon, Ohio, which he attended for two years.

In 1894 he joined two of his brothers, Sanson and James, in the real estate business in Cincinnati. After a few years of this joint effort he set up in business for himself, buying and selling real estate and constructing homes for sale, an activity in which he is still engaged. His other business interests, largely developed prior to his election as governor, include banking, lumber distribution, and coal mining.

Until Cooper became a candidate for governor in 1926, he had never run for public office. However, he had been identified closely

170

with Republican party politics in Cincinnati since the turn of the century. He campaigned for Taft in 1908, but joined the Bull Moose movement in 1912, returning to the regular Republican fold in 1916. He was a delegate to a state Republican party convention during the Hanna hegemony and has been elected either a district or state delegate to every Republican national convention since 1916 except in 1928, when he successfully campaigned for governor.

It is well known that party regularity and competence as an administrator alone are not sufficient qualifications to render a man available for nomination for state-wide office. Cooper had these; he also had become well known throughout Ohio from the fact that he had served eleven years as president of the Ohio Fair Managers Association and three terms as president of the Ohio Council of Churches. In addition, he conducted a successful primary campaign for the Republican gubernatorial nomination in 1926, losing in the election to the incumbent, Vic Donahey, by a scant 17,000 votes. This campaign took him to every part of the state and gave him a fine perspective on the needs of the state which might be met by the state government.

Cooper's plurality over the Democratic candidate, Martin L. Davey, in 1928, was overwhelming. It was a Republican year; Herbert Hoover went into the White House and all state offices in Ohio went to Republicans, except eleven members of the house of representatives. The stage was set for two years of unparalleled political harmony in the statehouse, which was all the more striking because of the contrast offered by Governor Donahey's incessant wrangling with the state legislature from 1923 to 1929.

The only session held by the eighty-eighth general assembly was short, adjourning on April 16, 1929; 222 bills were passed. The governor vetoed twenty-two and permitted three to become law without his signature. All the vetoes stuck. Every one of the eleven legislative recommendations made by the governor to the legislature became law. Among the principle legislative accomplishments were (1) repeal of the act permitting public utilities to put new rates into effect, pending their approval by the public utilities commission; (2) strengthening the investigative power of the public utilities commission; (3) strengthening the "Blue Sky" law; (4) revision of the general corporation act; (5) revision of the code of criminal procedure; (6) strengthening the election laws; (7) enactment of a law requiring permanent registration of voters; (8) reestablishment of the state library; (9) construction of the Departments of State Building; (10) enactment of a law for the conservation of natural resources; (11) creation of a state bureau of aeronautics; (12) strengthening the state banking laws; (13) consolidating parole services; (14) revising the highway code; and (15) providing for uniform veterans' guardianship.

Beyond this substantial accomplishment in new laws, one of the greatest achievements of the Cooper administration was its implementation of the financial provisions of the Reorganization Act of 1921, which had been largely disused by his predecessors. For the first time in state history the assembly had enough confidence in the governor to enact the biennial appropriation act in lump-sum form. The governor was given power to restrain expenditures through an allotment system, accrual accounting, and pre-auditing of expenditures. These were firmly and constructively used. The budget document prepared for 1931-32 was of a most modern type. State purchasing practices were revised and modernized. A complete new classification plan for the state civil service was prepared, although not in time for adoption—this step came only in 1949. Many other constructive accomplishments were recorded in all the broad area of state activities, including agriculture, commerce, public health, public welfare, highways, public works, education, and industrial relations.

The progressive and efficient service of the Cooper administration forms a bright chapter in the history of Ohio state government. However, the severe economic depression which paralyzed the world, heralded in the United States by the Wall Street crash of October 1929, has tended to overshadow the accomplishments of this period in the public memory. Those who know the history of the state government, however, trace many of the improved administrative practices now in use in the state to the Cooper period.

In the 1930 elections Governor Cooper was nominated by the Republicans without opposition, but lost to the Democratic candidate, George White, by 109,630 votes. This was a straw in the political wind that, in 1932, was to result in a Democratic national landslide. By that time it had become clear to all that depression, not recession, was the proper term for the economic situation. Those who occupied public office were among the victims.

After the inauguration of Governor White, Cooper returned to

Cincinnati, where he has continued with his successful business ventures and his service to his party, nation, state, and home community. In 1932 he again sought the Republican nomination for governor, but lost in the primary to David S. Ingalls of Cleveland, who, in turn, lost in the Democratic tide to Governor White. In 1936 he served as a member of the national Republican campaign staff. In 1938-41 he served as chairman of the committee on real estate taxation of the National Association of Real Estate Boards. During 1947-48 he was chairman of a commission appointed by Governor Thomas J. Herbert to select a new site for the Ohio Fair Grounds. Since 1933 he has been chairman of the Little Miami Conservancy District. In 1947 he served a one-year term as president of the National Exchange Clubs. During 1949-51 he was a member of Ohio's "Little Hoover Commission," which prepared for the consideration of the state government, proposals for administrative improvement and reform.

As one of Ohio's elder statemen he is much sought after for his mature wisdom on public questions. Already beyond the Biblical span, he remains vigorous and promises to serve his fellow citizens for additional years.

Governor Cooper's wife, Martha Kinney Cooper, is the founder of the Ohioana Library. The Coopers have two children, Raymond K. and Martha Ann.

The Ohio State University   HARVEY WALKER

GEORGE WHITE
1931 - 1935

George White, fifty-second governor of Ohio, was born in Elmira, New York, August 21, 1872, the elder of the two children of Charles W. and Mary (Back) White. His parents were natives of south-central New York, his father having been born at Havana (now Montour Falls) and his mother at Susquehanna. In 1873 the family moved to Titusville, Pennsylvania, where the father continued his work as a watchmaker and jeweler. George attended the public schools of Titusville, and in his spare time delivered newspapers and worked in stores. He went to Princeton University, where he had classes under Woodrow Wilson and from which he was graduated in 1895. After his graduation he worked in a lumber camp, as a roustabout in the oil fields of northwestern Pennsylvania, and as a school teacher. Then, early in 1898, he joined the gold rush to the Klondike.

As a gold seeker he packed an eight-hundred-pound outfit over the difficult Chilcoot Pass, "mushed" with sleds and dog teams, and labored at placer mining in the frozen Yukon subsoil. His experiences were later to enable him to speak with first-hand authority in congress

174

on the problems of Alaska, and to give him a slight air of exoticism on which he was able to capitalize politically. His financial rewards were more meager than popular report indicated. He once told a journalist that he had merely "picked up enough in the Klondike to buy a silk hat and a suit of clothes to get married in."

Immediately after his return from the gold fields he married Miss Charlotte McKelvy of Titusville on September 25, 1900. Shortly thereafter he moved to Woodsfield, Ohio, and then, in 1902, to Marietta. Here he entered the oil production business, first in Ohio and the nearby parts of West Virginia and later in Oklahoma. He returned to his highly successful enterprises in the intervals in his political life.

George White's first venture into politics was in 1905, when he was elected as a "dry" Democrat to represent normally dry Republican Washington County in the Ohio House of Representatives. He served on the temperance committee of the seventy-seventh general assembly (1906-8) and thereby strengthened his reputation as a "dry," but otherwise he was chiefly notable because he sponsored a joint resolution asking congress to submit a constitutional amendment providing for the direct election of United States senators.

The year after his election to the Ohio legislature, White obtained the Democratic nomination for the fifteenth congressional district, which had elected only Republicans since the Civil War. He lost to the incumbent, Beman G. Dawes, in November. He ran against James Joyce of Cambridge in 1908, and this time lost by only fifty-seven votes in 45,000. He defeated Joyce in 1910 and again in 1912. He lost to William C. Mooney of Woodsfield in 1914 by 104 votes, won over him in 1916 by 290 votes, and lost to C. Ellis Moore of Cambridge in 1918 by about 1,500 votes. As a member of the sixty-second, sixty-third, and sixty-fifth congresses, White served on the committees on pensions, mines and mining, and ways and means, voted twice for prohibition, and introduced the same joint resolution for the direct election of senators which he had already sponsored in the Ohio legislature.

During the political maneuvering which preceded the Democratic national convention of 1920, White supported his old congressional friend, Governor James M. Cox. He acted as chief assistant to Edward H. Moore, Cox's campaign manager, by maintaining an office in Washington to keep in touch with congressmen and visiting politicians. After Cox was nominated, White replaced Moore as campaign manager and was selected as Democratic national chairman in succession to Homer S. Cummings. He served acceptably in this capacity, conducting a clean rather than sensational campaign. Shortly after the Harding victory the forces in the Democratic party favorable to William Gibbs McAdoo tried to have White removed. At first they had little success, but finally, in November 1921, White resigned his office in the interests of party harmony and was replaced by Cordell Hull.

White next appeared on the political scene in 1928, when he lost the Democratic gubernatorial nomination to Charles V. Truax, state director of agriculture. Two years later he defeated Stephen M. Young in the primary, and then went on to beat Governor Myers Y. Cooper in November. In this election he apparently gained some advantage from his reputation as a "dry," but unquestionably his victory was primarily in the nature of a protest against the deepening economic depression. His reelection in 1932 over David Ingalls may, however, be taken as an endorsement of his conduct and policies as governor.

White's two terms as governor fell in the years of the trough of the national depression. His major activities and recommendations therefore related directly or indirectly to economic problems, such as falling state revenues, relief for the unemployed, and the crippling of the school system through the breakdown of the taxing capacity of the local subdivisions. He found it necessary to call three special sessions of the legislature in each of his terms. In general the legislature responded favorably to his suggestions.

White's attitude throughout was that the government must live within its means. He reduced state expenditures by eliminating certain services and having the legislature cut salaries on a graduated basis. Because existing sources of taxation, especially real estate taxes, bore unfairly on the rural population and failed to produce needed revenue, he advocated or accepted a series of new taxes, including a tax on intangibles, an excise tax on public utilities, taxes on cigarettes, beer, cosmetics, and amusement tickets, and, most important and controversial of all, a general retail sales tax of three percent. When the federal government commenced its emergency relief program in Ohio in 1933, White cooperated loyally with it and had the legislature enact laws paralleling or supplementing the national industrial recovery act and the agricultural adjustment act and providing for participation in the Muskingum Conservancy District. Other important if not spectacular legislation of his regime established a five-day waiting period for marriage licences, regulated fireworks, created the state highway patrol, set up the Ohio Milk Marketing Commission, and provided for a system of liquor control.

The chief emergencies with which White had to deal, other than unemployment and relief, concerned the banking crisis of 1933 and disorders in the coal mining regions. In the former, White was very reluctant to admit that the banks in Ohio needed to be closed, and when they were closed by the federal goverment, he had them reopened as soon as possible. In retrospect his handling of this problem appears very able. His position with reference to the coal field disorders was that the workers had a right to strike and should be protected in this right, but that he would not tolerate violence. Accordingly, he used the Ohio National Guard to maintain law and order, especially in Athens County. At the same time he attempted to mediate between the miners and owners, unfortunately with only temporary success.

White was given some consideration as a presidential and as a vice presidential possibility in 1932. He did not take his favorite-son candidacy very seriously, as is evidenced by a statement he made on the eve of the convention. "I am a fatalist," he said. "I believe whatever happens will be for the best." He nevertheless did write an open letter to former Senator Atlee Pomerene in which he revealed that he had changed his mind on the question of prohibition. He gave it as his opinion that prohibition was leading to disrespect for the law, and he suggested, therefore, that congress should recommend to the individual states the repeal of the Eighteenth Amendment and in the meantime should modify the Volstead act to legalize the manufacture and sale of beer. It should be emphasized that his letter did not represent mere expediency, for a few months earlier he had created a minor sensation in Ohio Anti-Saloon League circles by telling a convention of the Woman's Christian Temperance Union at Columbus much the same thing.

In January 1934, while he was still governor, White announced that he would seek the Democratic nomination for senator. Throughout his campaign he emphasized his loyalty to and his belief in the New Deal and in President Roosevelt, but the New Dealers were convinced —rightly enough—that he was not at heart one of them, and supported Assistant Secretary of the Interior Charles West. When James M. Cox and Senator Robert J. Bulkley endorsed West, White announced that he would not be "a rubber stamp" for Cox nor "an errand boy" for Bulkley. The claims and counterclaims as to whether White or West was the more loyal to the New Deal gave the impression that the contest was between them, but in the primary the third candidate, the personally popular non-New Dealer, Vic Donahey, won decisively.

White again attempted to gain the Democratic senatorial nomination in 1938, once more protesting his adherence to the New Deal. An aspect of the campaign which attracted much criticism was the fact that at the Northwest Territory Celebration at Marietta, President Roosevelt in his address failed to mention White (who was the chairman of the occasion) and did mention his New Deal rival Senator Bulkley, thus conveying the impression that he endorsed the latter. White was annoyed at what he considered a breach of good taste, but stated, at least for public consumption, that the mention of his rival did not do him any harm. It is doubtful if the endorsement, if such it was, was as important as was thought at the time. In any case, Bulkley went on to win the nomination easily.

Perhaps the most important outcome of this primary as far as White was concerned was that it marked his permanent alienation from Roosevelt and the New Deal. He had supported Roosevelt loyally in 1932 and, as he later said, with some mental reservations in 1936. He had cooperated fully with the national administration in its relief and conservation projects in Ohio. In return, the New Dealers had twice helped to bring about his defeat in the senatorial primary. Moreover, as a conservative White had been dubious of many of Roosevelt's ideas, and had been one of those opposing his scheme for the enlargement of the supreme court. When Roosevelt was nominated for a third term, it therefore occasioned no great surprise when White announced that he was a Jeffersonian Democrat and was bolting his party to support Wendell Willkie. When Roosevelt was reelected, he withdrew from politics.

George White was twice married. His first wife died in 1929. There were three sons (two now deceased) and two daughters of this marriage. In April 1936, he married Mrs. Agnes Hofman Baldwin of Parkersburg, West Virginia. There is one son of this marriage. White continued to live in Marietta, with the universal good will and esteem of the community, until his death on December 15, 1953.

Marietta College

ROBERT LESLIE JONES

MARTIN L. DAVEY
1935 - 1939

Martin L. Davey (July 25, 1884–March 31, 1946) was one of the early sponsors of network radio programs. Every weekend in the late 1920's he traveled from his home in Kent, Ohio, or his office in Washington, D. C., to New York City to personally supervise a Sunday afternoon program of music under the auspices of the Davey Tree Expert Company of which he was president. He, himself, selected the music to be played and delivered a short talk, generally about trees or about his father, John Davey, founder of the tree surgery business.

Any political advertising which Martin Davey received as a result of these programs was purely incidental. Or was it? For Davey was one of the most astute and thorough politicians of his time. He was then in congress. He had aspirations to become governor and perhaps president, and he always planned a long time in advance.

Davey was born in humble circumstances in Portage County. His father, who came from England to America in 1873, did not learn to read and write until he was twenty-one. But in 1901 he wrote a book,

The Tree Doctor, which became the inspiration for a profitable business which Davey carried on after his father's death, although his most intense interest was in politics.

Every Davey campaign began with letters to people on his mailing lists, and he had the most complete lists of Democratic voters and other groups ever assembled by an Ohio politician. As a candidate, Davey would ask their advice. As an officeholder he would tell them his problems. These letters served a double purpose. They not only pleased and flattered the recipients but they also provided Davey with an enthusiastic volunteer campaign organization.

One of Davey's favorite maxims was that "people vote their major prejudices." Consequently he always undertook to find out what those prejudices were, as far as his opponents were concerned, and to stimulate them on the theory that people would turn out with alacrity to vote against someone, whereas they might have to be dragged to the polls to vote for someone.

Davey had another theory, that a victor could always afford to be magnanimous. After a hard primary fight, in which he had denounced fellow Democrats with unequaled bitterness and thoroughness, he would set about methodically to appease the defeated candidates, making whatever concessions and promises were necessary to obtain their support.

After serving as mayor of Kent and a member of congress, Davey made his first try for governor in 1928, but was defeated. He did not try again until 1934, when he won, and then began one of the most extraordinary and bizarre periods in the annals of the Ohio governorship.

When the legislature refused to appropriate money to replace the threadbare rugs in the governor's office, Davey solicited contributions from the public and he got enough to recarpet the offices. When the legislature refused to appropriate money for a new limousine, he bought one with National Guard funds, observing that he had a right to do so because he was commander-in-chief of the Guard. When he wanted to get rid of the penitentiary warden, he had a National Guard company evict him and move his household belongings into the street.

Before he had been in office six weeks, Davey started a feud with President Roosevelt, charging that the federal administration of relief in Ohio was "cruel, inhuman and wasteful." Roosevelt struck back with the charge that there had been corrupt political interference with relief in Ohio, quoting Harry L. Hopkins, then federal relief administrator, as saying that Davey's campaign committee had extracted contributions from persons doing business with the Federal Relief Administration to finance Davey's inaugural ball. Davey countered by swearing out a warrant for Hopkins on a charge of criminal libel and, in an address to the legislature, asserting that Hopkins was a liar and a coward, and daring him to come into Ohio. He also demanded a legislative investigation, which disclosed that there had been a shakedown, but that it had not been engineered by Davey or his campaign committee but by some minor employees of the state relief administration who hoped to win promotions.

When Davey vetoed more than $10,000,000 in appropriations for Ohio State University, a Columbus newspaper mournfully predicted that the football schedule would have to be canceled because the university did not have enough money to buy coal to heat the athletic buildings. This brought a sarcastic statement from the governor to the effect that he realized football was the most important activity carried on at the university and disclaimed any desire to see the schedule curtailed. In fact, he said, he was so sympathetic toward the promotion of football that he had put half the members of the football squad on the state payroll. The repercussions from this one were heard from coast to coast.

In 1936 Davey grabbed a campaign issue which he thought would be popular. He asked the legislature to repeal the sales tax on food sold in stores for consumption off the premises. But by this time there was a full scale feud between the governor and the legislature, and it declined to act. Whereupon Davey had his own organization circulate petitions to put a constitutional amendment on the ballot, and it passed overwhelmingly. This measure has saved Ohioans millions of dollars a year in sales taxes. But Davey's detractors sneered that he had done it for a political motive, namely, to get reelected. He was reelected, and maybe the sales tax restriction helped, but Ohioans are still saving money by not having to pay the tax.

Davey's feud with the Roosevelt administration was suspended during the 1936 campaign, but it was resumed shortly thereafter when he called out the National Guard to maintain law and order during a steel strike in the Mahoning Valley. The strike was broken as a result, and Davey thereby incurred the undying enmity of John L. Lewis and the C. I. O., but he also got himself a law and order campaign issue.

When the C. I. O. attacked him, he countered with the charge that it was dominated by Communists. He also asserted that during the strike Roosevelt's secretary of labor, Frances Perkins, had called him and urged that he use the state's subpoena power to seize the steel company executives and lock them in a room until they agreed to sign a contract with the C. I. O.

During his second term Davey was in a constant feud with the senate "hatchet" men, a group of a dozen Democratic senators who were out to "get" him. With the help of five Republicans, who held the balance of power, they established a senate investigating committee which probed the Davey administration from stem to stern. Out of this investigation there came a succession of scandals which made lurid newspaper headlines, such as evidence of collusive bidding on the part of "hot mix" paving contractors and of the awarding of a trucking contract to a concern which had no trucks but was headed by a Democratic politician. Though these scandals never touched Davey personally, they had a bad effect on his political fortunes. When he ran for a third term in 1938 he was defeated for renomination by Charles Sawyer, formerly lieutenant governor and later secretary of commerce in the Truman administration. The Roosevelt administration contributed to his defeat by announcing three days before the primary that $1,300,000 in federal pension funds would be withheld from Ohio on the ground that Davey had sent political letters to old age pensioners.

After his defeat, Davey waited to be appeased as he had appeased so many other Democrats whom he had defeated. But the victorious Sawyer forces did not believe in being magnanimous. They ignored Davey and antagonized his supporters. This was conduct which, in Davey's book, called for punishment. Sawyer was defeated for election by John W. Bricker, the Republican candidate, whom Davey had defeated in 1936. Although the Davey forces did not openly support Bricker, there was no doubt that they contributed to Sawyer's defeat.

But the Sawyerites also got their revenge. In 1940, when Davey won the Democratic nomination in another try for a third term, they voted en masse for Bricker at the election, giving Davey the worst defeat any candidate for governor had suffered up to that time. This was his last appearance on the Ohio political scene. He retired to his home and business in Kent, where in 1946 he was stricken with a heart attack and died one evening while playing bridge with members of his family and friends. He was survived by his wife, the former Berenice Chrisman, and their two children.

Cleveland Plain Dealer   RALPH J. DONALDSON

JOHN W. BRICKER
1939 - 1945

The year 1938 saw the rebound of the Republican party in Ohio after eight years of Democratic rule in the statehouse and in most of the eighty-eight county courthouses—a period during which the party of Hayes, Garfield, McKinley, Hanna, and Foraker had ebbed to the lowest point of power since the Civil War. The candidate for governor who led the party to victory that year and who was twice reelected, thus becoming the first Republican governor to serve three consecutive terms, was John William Bricker.

Bricker was no "political accident." He had come up a long route of political activity, beginning with his indoctrination as a boy when he accompanied his father to the Republican party caucuses in his native Pleasant Township in Madison County. Politics was in his blood; he debated it in the high school at Mt. Sterling and as a member of the debating team at Ohio State University, where he divided his activities between forensics and the varsity baseball team. At the university, in 1916, he organized a campus club supporting Hughes and Willis, the candidates for president and governor. While yet in his twenties, he was elected president of the Buckeye Republican Club of Columbus. By that time many party members already had their eyes on him as a "young hopeful" among Republicans. Years later one of the state's best-known Republican leaders of Ohio said: "I have never known anyone except Bricker whose friends have thought from the time he was 18 years old that he would some day be governor."

John Bricker was born on September 6, 1893, in a house built partly of logs on a small farm, the son of Lemuel and Laura King Bricker. On his paternal side he was descended from colonial settlers who came to Maryland from southern Germany; on his mother's side he was of Scotch-Irish descent, also by way of Maryland. Bricker and his twin sister, Ella, later Mrs. P. Freeman Mooney, attended one-room rural schools in Madison County until they entered Mt. Sterling High School.

Bricker's college career was interrupted by World War I in which he served as a chaplain in the army. Because of a "slow heart," he had been rejected by the army, the navy, and the marines, and finally by his draft board. By special ordination of his church, the Christian, the way was opened for him to enter the army chaplain corps. Shortly before the armistice in 1918, he was approved for line service, the physical requirements having been changed, but with the cessation of hostilities the transfer fell through and he was mustered out of the service as a first lieutenant in the chaplain corps.

Bricker's first public office (1920) was that of solicitor of the village of Grandview, a Columbus suburb. Three years later he was appointed assistant attorney general and counsel for the Public Utilities Commission of Ohio, in which position he was soon established as a champion of fair utilities prices for the consumer. In 1928, at the age of thirty-four, Bricker became a candidate for attorney general and missed nomination by less than 8,800 votes in a field of six. The next year Governor Myers Y. Cooper named Bricker to the public utilities commission where, during three years of service, he made a distinguished record as an advocate of fair rates and the extension and improvement of utilities services in rural areas. He was nominated for attorney general without opposition in 1932, and was elected despite the fact that the Democratic governor, George White, was reelected by a plurality of more than 200,000 and that Franklin D. Roosevelt carried the state for president.

His record as attorney general was such as to merit reelection, and he was elected by a plurality of 40,000, again in the face of a general Democratic sweep throughout Ohio. By 1936 it was almost universally conceded that Bricker should be the Republican candidate for governor, and he was nominated without opposition to face the Democratic incumbent, Martin L. Davey, who was seeking a second term. That year the national administration of Franklin D. Roosevelt was at its height of popularity and power. Under the existing Ohio election code, the national and state tickets were printed on the same ballot, and Governor Davey made the most of that fact, tying his candidacy to that of Roosevelt. Bricker attempted to press home charges of waste and corruption in the state government, but the Davey strategy won, the Democrats winning every state office and the general assembly. Bricker, however, ran 300,000 votes ahead of the presidential nominee and it was a foregone conclusion he would again lead his party's ticket in 1938. In the latter year, Bricker campaigned vigorously and effectively, sometimes traveling several hundred miles a day. During the legislative sessions of 1937 and 1938, a senate committee of the Democratic legislature had produced testimony supporting the charges Bricker had made in the 1936 campaign regarding the Davey administration. Davey was defeated for renomination by Charles Sawyer, a former lieutenant governor and at that time the Democratic national committeeman from Ohio. Bricker drove home the campaign slogan, "Ohio Needs a Change," and won by a majority of 118,229, leading to victory a list of candidates, including Robert A. Taft, first Republican United States Senator from Ohio in ten years, and fifteen out of twenty-four members of the national house of representatives from Ohio, and enough Republican candidates for the legislature to return that body to Republican control.

In his inaugural address, delivered on January 9, 1939, Governor Bricker spoke out against the growing centralization of government and the growing dependence on federal bureaucracy. "There must be a revitalization of state and local governments throughout the nation," he said. "The individual citizen must again be conscious of his responsibility to his government and alert to the preservation of his rights as a citizen under it. That cannot be done by taking government further away, but by keeping it at home. . . . Here in America we are determined again to encourage business rather than to hinder it; to preserve opportunity and to recognize the proper place of the individual in his government.

. . . No superman or dictator can point the way to the better life we seek. It is a democratic task. The leadership must be of the many, of people of high character and good purpose. Such leadership is undramatic but safe. By it, democracies can serve and build."

This was Bricker's political creed. It ruled his conduct during his six years as governor; it was his platform as a candidate for the Republican nomination for president in 1944, and the theme that pervaded the hundreds of speeches he made that year in a transcontinental tour as his party's candidate for vice president, following his nomination to that office by the Republican national convention; it is the philosophy to which he has adhered as United States Senator from Ohio, since his election to that office in 1946 and his reelection in 1952.

When Bricker assumed the governorship of Ohio in 1939, the state was operating under a $40,000,000 deficit, composed mostly of promises made to local subdivisions, including school districts, to pay off debts the state had authorized them to incur in lieu of a balanced state budget. Governor Bricker at once instituted a program of economy which included dismissal of hundreds of unnecessary state employes, cancellation of contracts for state supplies in favor of agreements at lower prices, reorganization of various departments of state government, revamping of state and local government budget procedures, and enforcement of tax laws as to assessments and collections. This program resulted, during Bricker's six years as governor, not only in the liquidation of the debts incurred by schools and local governments and in the erasure of a $2,000,000 operating deficit, but in the accumulation of a surplus in excess of $90,000,000. At the same time, payments in old age pensions were substantially increased, partly by larger state appropriations; the state public school foundation program was put in operation in its entirety for the first time; many state and local facilities were provided for defense purposes from the state treasury; a post-war building fund of $19,000,000 for state institutions was established; local government debts were decreased; and the efficiency and services of the state departments were improved generally. Each of the times the voters reelected Bricker governor, that is, in 1940 and 1942, it was by an increased majority.

Most of the period of World War II fell within Bricker's administration. Advance planning under his direction enabled Ohio to slip into wartime gear with a minimum of strain and confusion. Months before Pearl Harbor, the governor had appointed a committee to coordinate industrial activities with national defense and had obtained from the legislature authorization for a state council of defense and local defense councils, an increase in the size of the state highway patrol; and the establishment of a state guard to defend the state in the absence of the Ohio National Guard which had been called into federal service in October 1940. Through these agencies and the regular departments of the state government, Ohio was well prepared for the demands of wartime. After Pearl Harbor it was unnecessary even to call a special session of the legislature. Bricker's appointments of commanding officers in the Ohio National Guard were shown by their performance and record in World War II to have been exceptionally outstanding.

Mrs. Bricker, the former Harriet Day of Urbana, a fellow student of Bricker's at Ohio State, was one of the most charming and beloved of Ohio's "first ladies." The Brickers have an adopted son, John Day Bricker.

Ohio State Journal   KARL B. PAULY

FRANK J. LAUSCHE
1945 - 1947, 1949-

When the smoke of battle of the hectic political campaign of 1952 cleared away, the people of Ohio beheld an amazing result. Governor Frank J. Lausche, running for an unprecedented fourth term as Ohio's chief executive, had won reelection by the record-breaking margin of approximately 425,000 votes over his Republican opponent, Charles P. Taft. This was in the face of a national Republican landslide which saw General Dwight D. Eisenhower carry Ohio by a half million votes and a state-wide Republican sweep which carried to victory every other state Republican candidate.

By his spectacular triumph Governor Lausche made political history in Ohio. Not only did he become the first four-term governor in Ohio's 150 years of statehood, but, in addition, his incredible total vote of 2,019,029, made him the first Ohioan ever to receive as many as two million votes for any office in the state, and his margin of victory set a record as the greatest plurality ever accorded an Ohio governor.

Lausche, born of immigrant parents in the grimy steel mill district

189

of Cleveland on November 14, 1895, had indeed come a long way. His father, a steel mill worker, and his mother, who befriended all new arrivals in the neighborhood, had a family of ten children, of whom Frank was the second. The father and the oldest son died when Frank was twelve years old. To help support the family, Frank sold newspapers on the street corners of Cleveland, became the neighborhood lamplighter at two dollars a week, and helped his mother operate a small restaurant and wine shop. He also found time to play baseball and soon became a star sand-lot third baseman. For a time he played semi-professional baseball with Duluth in the Northern League and with Lawrence, Massachusetts, in the Eastern League.

During World War I Lausche joined the army as a private in 1918, and rose to the rank of second lieutenant. On his return from service in 1919, he passed up a bid to play professional baseball in order to study law. He entered John Marshall Law School in Cleveland, and, upon completion of his law studies in 1920, he passed the Ohio bar examination with the second highest grade in the state. He then entered the practice of law as an assistant in the law firm headed by Cyrus Locher, who became a United States Senator in 1928. It was on the advice of Locher that Lausche became a candidate for the Ohio legislature. Although he met defeat in the campaigns of 1922 and 1924, he made a favorable impression on his party chiefs, and he became the Democratic ward leader in his neighborhood.

In 1932 Governor White appointed Lausche to fill a vacancy on the Cleveland municipal bench. He served in this office with distinction and was reelected. In 1936 he was elected to the common pleas bench and quickly achieved a solid reputation as a courageous, industrious, and nonpolitical judge. Lausche used his powers as judge to gather evidence against gambling clubs in Cuyahoga County and to have warrants sworn out against their operators. In so doing he offended political leaders of his party, and it was predicted that Lausche had committed political suicide. But the gambling clubs were closed, and Lausche's reputation spread, with the result that in 1941, when he ran for mayor of Cleveland, he was elected by the largest majority and with the greatest percentage of votes ever given a municipal candidate in Cleveland.

Hardly had Lausche assumed his duties as mayor of Cleveland when World War II broke out. In addition to his usual functions as mayor, he assumed direction of all protective facilities and of all efforts to win the war on the home front. He mobilized volunteers to plan for a county-wide program and raised money to pay the bill. His success with these achievements gained for him a national reputation as "an inspired war leader for the people of Cleveland." In 1943 he was reelected mayor by an even greater majority than in his first victory. His reputation as an able administrator spread throughout Ohio, and in 1944 he was elected governor of Ohio in a campaign in which he was opposed by James Garfield Stewart, mayor of Cincinnati.

Lausche's towering and commanding figure, with a great mop of black hair that waved about when he warmed up on the platform, became a familiar figure to Ohio voters. They liked his home-folksy manner, and his pleasant, even disposition and infectious smile. He impressed his hearers as being utterly sincere and honest in his deep attachment to the principles of democracy and clean government. They liked his independence of pressure groups, and incidentally they liked the charming, friendly, and gracious Mrs. Lausche, the former Jane Sheal, whom Lausche had married in 1928. And they elected him as the state's fifty-fifth governor by a majority of 112,359 votes.

A national Republican landslide was chiefly responsible for Lausche's defeat by Thomas J. Herbert in the election of November 1946. But two years later he was swept back into office over Governor Herbert. Subsequently, in the election of November 1950 and in the face of a strong Republican trend, Lausche's great popularity with the people brought him his third election as governor—this time by 150,000 votes over Don H. Ebright. Thus Lausche became the fifth Ohio governor to be elected to a third term.

In 1952, when he became a candidate for an unprecedented fourth term, opponents made a point of the fact that no other governor in Ohio's history had asked the voters for four terms. His ensuing record-breaking victory was all the more impressive because of the stature of his opponent who bore the magic political name of Taft—capable, personable, and independent Charles Phelps Taft, the son of President William Howard Taft and the brother of the famous late Senator Robert A. Taft.

Although the general assembly was usually dominated by the opposite party during the Lausche administrations, Governor Lausche was exceptionally successful in having much of his program adopted. Among the outstanding contributions of his administrations was the program for the conservation and restoration of the state's natural resources, including legislation requiring strip-mine operators to reclaim spoil banks and the governor's voluntary "Plant Ohio" campaign.

All phases of the state's welfare program were greatly expanded under his administration, with state expenditures in that field in the fiscal year 1952-53 reaching a total of $97,405,726. At many state institutions improvements were made in existing facilities and new buildings were constructed. The latter include modern hospital buildings at Applecreek, Lima, and Tiffin state hospitals. After a serious riot at the Ohio State Penitentiary, October 31-November 3, 1952, which dramatically demonstrated the overcrowded conditions in the state's penal institutions, the governor called a conference of welfare officials and legislative leaders to develop a plan for prison improvement. To implement this program the 100th general assembly appropriated $8,-500,000 to augment the $5,000,000 program then under way. Several new buildings at various penal institutions have been completed, and the first unit of the new Marion Training School for older delinquent youths, a $3,250,000 building, is under construction.

Expansion programs were developed in all of the state's institutions of higher learning, and a huge medical center was opened on the campus of the Ohio State University in November 1951. Governor Lausche was criticized for his reluctance to recommend higher appropriations from the general revenue fund for the support of public schools. He advocated greater support and control by local school districts.

In 1949 the legislature voted to float a bond issue for the construction of a turnpike across Ohio to connect with the Pennsylvania turnpike. A bond issue of $500,000,000 was approved by popular referendum in November 1953 to finance a long-term highway improvement program commensurate with the requirements of present-day traffic. The cost of amortization of the bonds is to be met by the gasoline tax and a new weight-distance tax on trucks. The governor enforced this tax in the face of much opposition, believing it to be the fairest form of assessment for highway use. The governor called a special session of the assembly in December 1951 and appointed a highway commission to deal with highway problems and administration.

In May 1949 the governor approved a law providing for a civil defense organization. Under this law the governor appointed an advisory defense council and set up a defense organization throughout the state.

As ex-officio chairman of the council he assumed active direction of the organization and made Ohio one of the leading states in this field. His leadership was recognized nationally by appointment to the president's advisory council of governors.

In 1949 the assembly authorized the appointment of a sesquicentennial commission to plan the observance of the state's 150th anniversary. The governor appointed a commission headed by Harvey Firestone, Jr., and served as an ex-officio member of the commission. During 1953 he made numerous speeches and appearances throughout the state in connection with the celebration.

Throughout his administrations Governor Lausche waged a continual warfare upon commercialized gambling and racketeering in Ohio.

Governor Lausche's great popularity with the voters and his achievements as Ohio's chief executive made him a national figure. President Roosevelt appointed him a member of a national committee to investigate alleged racial discrimination in the South, and in 1950 he was elected chairman of the Governors' Conference of the United States.

The life of Frank J. Lausche, the son of immigrant parents who became Ohio's first and only four-term governor, is an American success story. This fact was dramatically recognized when Western Reserve University presented him the honorary degree of Doctor of Laws on June 11, 1951. The citation read: "Frank J. Lausche, jurist, public servant and demonstrator that America is still the land of opportunity."

Juvenile Court of Cuyahoga County　　　　ALBERT A. WOLDMAN

————

Since the sketch of Governor Lausche was set in type, he has been elected to a fifth term as governor by a majority of approximately 215,000 over his opponent, James A. Rhodes, auditor of state.

THE EDITORS

THOMAS J. HERBERT
1947 - 1949

The Republican landslide in Ohio in 1946 brought to the office of chief executive of the state as Ohio's fifty-sixth governor, Thomas J. Herbert, who was well known to Ohio voters, having served as attorney general for three terms.

Herbert was born in Cleveland on October 28, 1894. His parents, John T. and Jane Jones Herbert, were both descendants of Welsh settlers of Jackson County, Ohio, where his four grandparents and eight great grandparents all are buried.

After graduation from the public schools of Cleveland, Thomas Herbert attended Adelbert College, Western Reserve University, and Western Reserve University Law School, graduating from the former in 1915 and from the latter in June 1920. His legal education was interrupted by military service in World War I. He enrolled in the first officers' training school at Fort Benjamin Harrison, and after a period of training there and at Ohio State University, he volunteered to fly in Italy. He did not reach Italy, however, but served as a first lieutenant in the United States air forces, attached to the 56th British Royal Air Force squadron. On his third mission, while giving air support to Allied forces at Belleau Wood, he was shot down and wounded August 8, 1918, at Cambrai, France. Hospitalized for two years, he was honorably discharged in May 1920, after having reentered law school while still walking with crutches. He was awarded the British Distinguished Flying Cross, the American Distinguished Service Cross, and the Purple Heart for his heroism in service.

Herbert was admitted to the bar in December 1919, and in 1921 he began his public career as assistant director of law for the city of Cleveland. He was next appointed assistant prosecuting attorney for Cuyahoga County, serving two years, 1922-23. His first state office was that of assistant attorney general of Ohio, in which position he was assigned as attorney for the Public Utilities Commission of Ohio, 1929-33. In 1936 he ran on the Republican ticket for the office of attorney general, but lost the contest by 280,000 votes in the election in which Alfred Landon, the Republican presidential candidate, lost Ohio by a staggering total of 620,000. He sought the Republican nomination for governor in 1944, but lost out by 2,000 votes to James G. Stewart, who in turn lost the election to Frank J. Lausche. Two years later, however, Herbert won the nomination and the election, administering the only defeat Governor Lausche has met in his five campaigns for the governorship. In 1948 the tables were turned, and Lausche won over Herbert by a substantial majority.

During Governor Herbert's administration, 1947-49, a number of constructive measures were enacted at the governor's urging or with his approval. Most important, in the governor's opinion, were six bills reducing or eliminating certain taxes (the tax on sales amounting to less than forty-one cents was rescinded), with a saving to the taxpayers of $86,000,000 and two bills appropriating a total of $45,000,000 from the surplus in the treasury for compensation to World War II veterans.

His administration inaugurated and nearly completed a large building construction program in the welfare department. The Mount Vernon State Hospital for the tuberculous mentally ill, the only one in the United States, was dedicated by Governor Herbert in 1947. Much progress was made also in the departments of health, industrial relations, and agriculture. Agriculture benefitted especially because of the improved plant and animal disease control program. School appropriations were increased approximately $49,000,000 over those of the previous administration. His administration was responsible for paving more miles of new road and resurfacing more miles of old road than in any previous biennium. Governor Herbert placed inspectors in the liquor department under classified civil service for the first time and eliminated surplus liquor stocks from the inventory. He courageously vetoed the popular Van Aken labor bill because he believed it unworkable and detrimental to the best interests of both labor and management. Governor Herbert proved himself a wise and resourceful leader. Mild in manner and unassuming, he was capable of aggressive action when he deemed it necessary.

Thomas Herbert was married in 1919 to Jeannette Judson, who died in 1945, leaving a daughter and two sons. The daughter, Mrs. Charles Lewis Stevers, was hostess for her father at the executive mansion until his marriage on January 3, 1948, to Miss Mildred Stevenson of Indianapolis, Indiana, who became a gracious first lady. At the close of his term the governor returned to Cleveland and engaged in the private practice of law. In May 1953 he was appointed by President Eisenhower a member of the Subversive Activities Control Board. He was made chairman of the board and has his headquarters in the Lafayette Building in Washington, D. C.

The Ohio Historical Society   S. WINIFRED SMITH

W Dennison Jr.

Thos. L. Young

Eedward

Jno. Brough

R. Lucas

J. B. Tod

Frank B. Willis

Geo. Hoo

Othniel Looker

Jno. K. Nash

Othao

Tho. Corwin

Thomas J. Herbert

Wilson Shannon

Lem Huntington

Wm

Duncan McArthur

James E.

Tho.

A. L. Harris

Seabury Ford

Richard M. Bishop

John M. Pattison

Martin

T Worthington

J. B. Foraker

Allen Trimble

Asa S. Bu

Hoyt —
James M. Co.
Vic. Donahey
R. B. Hayes
Upson Smith
Jeremiah Morrow
R. Wood
Harry L. Davis
Marley ? Raruche
Mn. Bartley
Wm. McKinley
Judson Harmon
Allen Trimble
Wm Bebb
Joseph Vance
Kirker
Edward Tiffin
Charles Anderson
Ulysses ? Draper
Charles Foster
John L. Baker
H. Allen
Robert Lucas